To Elaine Paris.
May the silen... lead you more fully into life!
May you follow your deep calling

Awakening:

A Contemplative Primer on Learning to Sit

By Nancy Flinchbaugh

Nancy Flinchbaugh
2020

Higher Ground Books & Media
Springfield, Ohio.
http://www.highergroundbooksandmedia.com

Printed in the United States of America 2020

Awakening:

A Contemplative Primer on Learning to Sit

By Nancy Flinchbaugh

TABLE OF CONTENTS

BEGINNING MATTERS

Accolades for *Awakening*

Awakening is a friendly and accessible introduction to a variety of contemplative practices, but even more than that, it offers a truly holistic approach to a deeply earthy, embodied spirituality. If you want to connect the dots between mind and body, between spirit and matter, and between contemplation and action, this book will show you the way.

— Carl McColman, author of *The Big Book of Christian Mysticism*

A valuable and lucid contribution to understanding many basic practices and understanding of Christian contemplatively grounded living.

— Tilden Edwards, author of *Embracing the Call to Spiritual Depth* and the founder of Shalem Institute for Spiritual Formation

This book is a wonderful, thoughtful and unique introduction to the art of contemplation. I learned a lot of things and found it very easy reading.

— Ken Whitt, author of *Halfway to Heaven*

Letters from the Earth author Nancy Flinchbaugh delves into the next step of not only appealing for preserving Earth, but also sharing her spiritual journey to experience the universal love of our Creator, appropriately titled "Awakening." She shares her methods of yoga postures, walking through a labyrinth of chakras, prayers, contemplation and meditation. She extends her experience with a wider group of Christians and people of other faiths due to her inclusive belief and respect for humanity and all beings who are part of Creation.

— Ravi Khanna, M.D.,
Hindu Physician

DEDICATION

This book is dedicated

to all of you

who seek to be awakened

and is offered with a prayer

that your awakening

will unfold into bountiful transformations,

within your life,

your community and

our world.

Introduction: A Message from the Author

In this post-modern world, we are beginning to sense that something is wrong with the frenzy of activity in which we dwell. Many sense we are on a collision course with the life of our planet. Our churches seek to provide a relevant alternative, a pathway to a deep spirituality that will help us make sense of our reality and connect us to Living Water, the fountain of all blessing that will energize and help us create possible futures together.

During this time, the contemplative path emerges to lead us home into the mystery and the hope of all creation. Christians have much to learn from the mystics within our own tradition and even from the mystical threads in other spiritual traditions.

This contemplative primer offers readers the opportunity to dwell in simple presence. Although not a complicated path, one must slow down and commit to the discipline of listening and silence to enter that sacred spaciousness of God. Whether you practice for one hour or the rest of your life, the exercises in this book prompt you to taste the goodness of contemplative space. As you cultivate this stillness in the center of your being, your life will begin to unfold into the beauty for which you were created.

The contemplative gifts build on each other and offer a path deep into the love of God. There are many ways to listen and to enter the silence. But once there, the experience grows over time into an incredible journey.

After some introductory background, the book follows a simple pattern of introducing a contemplative gift, a Letter from the Earth about that practice, my personal thoughts on the practice from my experience, suggestions for personal practice and then a plan for a group session on the practice, because many find contemplative practice enhanced in a group. These group sessions follow a rhythm of introduction, body prayer, silence and reflection leading into the holy space of God's presence.

We begin with the practice of "Simply Sitting," the entry point into Christian contemplative practice. Although this can be difficult for both beginners and experienced meditators alike, most who stick with a meditation practice report it's very helpful. For me, it's become a necessary part of my day, which illumines and transforms both my inner self and my experience of life in so many ways. As each day begins, my meditation practice calms me, connects me with God, and helps me prepare to serve while dwelling in the miracle of life unfolding moment by moment.

We move on to a form of walking meditation, the Labyrinth. This ancient practice finds new life in our era, helping us connect with God and the Earth.

Next, we'll explore the gift of sacred conversation. Finding a faithful friend, a spiritual director and/or a small group can be so helpful on your contemplative journey. A relationship of deep listening may lead you into growth as you encounter the many challenges and joys of life.

Then, we'll consider three contemplative practices that may be entry points to a time of meditation each day. 1. Gratitude helps acknowledge joy in life. 2. *Lectio Divina* with Scripture teaches a method of listening to sacred scripture with the heart. 3. *Lectio Divina* with the Earth listens for God speaking through marvels of nature.

Another contemplative gift discussed comes in the possibilities around mealtime and food. Mindful eating slows you down, as you savor food and consider the miracles in digestion and the process of food production. You might also lose weight!

Contemplative group rituals provide yet another entry to sacred space. We'll discuss the Taize movement in this section.

Next, we'll explore possibilities for contemplative practice throughout each day as we consider easing our whole self into a contemplative lifestyle.

I write from a Christian perspective, but I also find that the contemplative life unites us with those in other spiritual traditions, as we meet in the silence. I've included in this book how my Christian faith informs my contemplative practice, and also how some of my friends enter contemplative practice through the portals of their faith – Farzana Moon as a Muslim in the Sufi tradition, Ravi Khanna as a Hindu, Debra Williamson as a Buddhist, and Jagdish Singh as a Sikh, offer parallel practice to mine.

Within Christianity there are many varieties of contemplative practice, so I include the perspective of my friend, Therese Taylor-Stinson, as a person of color within the Christian tradition in this section. She helps me realize that I have been largely influenced by a white "European" Christian perspective. Within the African-American Christian tradition, contemplation takes on many other forms not discussed in this book. I think an additional primer is needed to explore the many ways that an oppressed culture finds ways to draw closer to God through music, rituals of prayer, interpretation of scripture to explain their struggle and lead them into future. Barbara Holmes, in her book, *Joy Unspeakable: Contemplative Practices of the Black Church, 2nd edition* (2017), explores the very important contemplative practices within the slave culture and the Black church. She notes that the civil rights movement emerged and was sustained by these contemplative practices. In this tradition, silence may be present, but this contemplation also happens within lively communal musical and prayer events which lead into the spaciousness of God's love. Also, when members of the dominant culture silence those they oppress, silence becomes a practice to resist. Rather, she notes deep contemplative practice within the culture of those oppressed must be connected with action. I share with her the perspective that contemplation is indelibly linked with action. As Therese Taylor-Stinson has said, "Silence for the oppressed should be embraced on their own terms and their more kataphatic[1] ways of being and prayer

---

[1]Therese Taylor-Stinson. "Silence and the Oppressed." Next Church Blog, https://nextchurch.net/silence-and-the-oppressed, 2019. In this blog, Taylor-Stinson distinguishes between apophatic and kataphatic prayer. "Apophatic prayer is a willing surrender into mystery: that which cannot be fully known and is closer to the true nature of God. It means emptying the mind of words and ideas and simply resting in the presence of the unknown. Kataphatic prayer, on the other hand, has

embraced more fully by contemplatives of every culture, unless it remains a tool to keep the narrative of the oppressed untold." (See her Blog Post "Silence and the Oppressed" (Taylor-Stinson, 2019).[2]

Finally, it's my belief that our awakening into contemplative practice leads to centered action and service in the Christian life. While meditation finds value in the present moment, it also prepares us for the adventure of a faith in practice. We will consider how we are called to use gifts and skills in areas of passion to make this world a better place.

I pray this book will be a tool for all of us to use both alone and with groups as we seek a path of contemplative practice, close to the heart of God. Because I find this practice very transformative and helpful to me in my daily life, I feel a call to share it with others.

Nancy Flinchbaugh
Springfield, Ohio

1/12/20

---

content; it uses words, images, symbols, and ideas. Ignatian prayer, such as lectio divina, the daily examen, and the Ignatian process for discernment. Other forms may be writing, music, dance, and other art forms."

[2] Taylor-Stinson, Therese. "Silence and the Oppressed," 2019. Op. Cit.

About Letters from the Earth

Letters from the Earth

Received by Nancy Flinchbaugh

Let me say a word about the "Letters from the Earth," included for each contemplative practice. I am very concerned about our changing climate. When I read *Active Hope* by Joanna Macy and Chris Brownstone[3] several years ago, they suggested writing a letter to yourself from the Earth. When I tried doing this, I found the letter to be quite delightful. I continued the practice, and it's been so helpful to me in my life. I really believe these letters come from deep in the heart of God, the nurturing energy in all of creation. Although they come through me, they always take me a little further than where I am. I find myself thinking, I never thought of it that way before. I wrote the first 24 of them into a memoir, *Letters from the Earth* by Nancy Flinchbaugh (2018).[4] You can also read many of the letters on my website at spiritualseedlings.com. So, for this primer on

---

[3]Joanna Macy and Chris Brownstone. *Active Hope: How to Face the Mess We're in without Going Crazy.* Novato, California: New World Library, 2012.

[4]Flinchbaugh, Nancy. *Letters from the Earth.* (Springfield, Ohio: Higher Ground Books and Media, 2018

contemplative practices, I decided to listen and receive Letters from the Earth to seek wisdom on the various topics in this book. When she writes, she addresses me personally by name. However, in this book I have changed "Nancy" to "Dear One" because she also encourages me to share these letters with others. She usually signs her letters, "Gaia." For me, that speaks to God's presence within all of the magnificent creation. I hope you will enjoy the female language for God, which helps balance the male language that is much more common, at least in the Christian church. I believe God transcends gender.

A Word about Definitions

Many words can be used to explain spiritual practices. The following definitions help explain the use of these words in this book.

Contemplative Practice – A variety of practices that help cultivate inner silence. Meditation, labyrinth walking, *Lectio Divina* with scripture and the Earth, mindful eating, contemplative action are all contemplative practices.

Meditation – The practice of sitting or walking into silence.

Body Prayer – A process of focusing on the body which can be helpful leading into a time of meditation.

Lectio Divina – A process to focus on scripture, sacred words and/or the Earth. There are four steps, defined with Latin words. 1) *Lectio.* Read. This step involves carefully listening, reading slowly and meditatively for what shimmers. 2) *Meditatio.* Reflect. This step involves reflecting on what the word, phrase or aspect shimmered for you and what significance this holds for you in your life. How is it speaking to you? Although the Latin word sounds like "meditation", this is not a time of letting go of thoughts. Rather, you want to ruminate on the shimmering message for you. 3) *Oratio.* Pray. During this step, you pray about whatever you've discovered. You ask God to help you in applying it to your life. This is usually a silent prayer, involving a petition to God. 4) *Contemplativo.* Meditate into silence. During this step, you sit in silence, what we would call "meditating." Again, the Latin word is somewhat confusing, because it sounds like contemplative. The word has various connotations in English, but here in *Lectio Divina*, it means to meditate into silence, letting go of words.

On Group Practice

Many find practicing meditation and other contemplative practices heightened when experienced with others in a group setting. Contemplative groups also help teach the practices for personal spiritual discipline. If you can find others interested in meeting weekly for contemplative prayer, you should do so. Your contemplative journey will be enhanced by sharing it with others in community.

Finding a space where you can be uninterrupted and enjoy silence is very important. Perhaps a room in your church, a library, community center, or someone's living room. Arrange the chairs in a circle. Put a candle in the center and perhaps a plant or flower.

Take some time in your group to agree on logistics. When will you meet and for how long? Who will lead the sessions? If possible, take turns leading and arranging the space. A simple structure, as demonstrated in the contemplative exercises in this book, works well. You might want to begin with a short checking-in, letting each person say a sentence or two about how they are doing, and then move into a time of body prayer, followed by a time of silence and journaling. Afterwards, you can have a time of discussion, sharing and group prayer. Some groups read books to help guide their practice.

I recommend setting ground rules for the sharing time. Some rules to consider are:

- Listen attentively.

- Honor the spaces between the words. (This means to agree to allow silence at times while people are speaking. Don't rush to complete sentences.)

- Let each other finish before you speak.

- Value differences.

- Seek authenticity in self and others.

- Use "I" statements rather than "we" or "they."

- Commit to confidentiality.

- Self-disclosure should be appropriate to the trust level, and it's always okay to pass.

- Respect time and timing.

- Avoid discussion, debate, or problem-solving.

- Feel free to ask for silence at any time, trusting others will value this opportunity for attending to Spirit.

You also may want to consider combining your contemplative prayer group with a common mission. The life of prayer leads into action. Action leads back into a need for prayer. Could your group be a prayer and action group? If so, part of your time could also be devoted to planning your mission work. You might consider adding contemplative practice to a mission group you're already involved in such as running a food pantry, community meals, mission trips to another country, a soup kitchen, a second-hand store, making quilts for others, etc. Or you might call people together to start a new mission and use the contemplative practice suggestions for groups as you begin to meet. Is there a project you've been wanting to start such as offering a listening space in the community, providing hospitality to re-entry citizens, or offering tutoring and/or mentoring to young people?

A group could initially form to work through the contemplative practices in this book, reading a chapter before each meeting. After finishing the book, you could rotate back through the practices or settle on the ones the group members enjoy the best. Or another approach would be to use the practices in a retreat setting, inviting the author or another contemplative leader to guide your retreat.

AWAKENING

Gary Geis School of Dance students present "Lion King, Jr." at the John Legend Theater, Springfield, Ohio

Awaken

Awaken, body of mine.

    Be here now.

    Feel heart beating.

Sense lungs breathing.

    Open eyes and ears.

    Move into space, dancing, laughing, loving.

    Be miraculously alive.

Awaken, mind of mine.

> *Think into now.*

> *Synapses connecting.*

> *Information assembling.*

> *Intelligence surging.*

> *Open all possibilities.*

> *Move into inventive solutions, hope for tomorrow.*

> *Be highest consciousness of Planet Earth.*

Awaken, Spirit within.

> *Connecting to You, Oh God.*

> *Feeling Presence.*

Sensing Love.

> *Hearing with Your ears, seeing with Your eyes.*

> *Moving into Your plans, Your hopes, Your path.*

> *May I connect with You, Creator of all.*

Gull alert at daybreak on Surfside Beach, S.C.

"We will go into the future as a single sacred community, or we will all perish in the desert."   *- Thomas Berry*

During this time, I believe we are all called to awaken. Planet Earth needs all of us now. Some suggest that we humans are Creation's pinnacle. We do hold the intelligence to lead our species into healing the planet, but we must awaken to this urgency. We must summon all of our abilities as the miraculous beings we are and work together.

This book offers not just a way to assist the reader and groups to enter into the silence, but also a call to move out from the silence, awakened to what

Thomas Berry calls our "Great Work."[5] He also coined the term, "The Ecozoic Age,"[6], in which humans must change their relationship with the Earth and work to preserve life here. The Earth will survive, humans may not. Don't we owe it to our Creator and the future of our species, to awaken and put all of our intelligence, resources and energy into moving into a new relationship with our Earth, a sustainable plan for life?

---

[5] *Thomas Berry, The Great Work: Our Way into the Future.* New York City, New York: Broadway Books, 2000, p. 85. Ecozoic Age reference

[6]Ecozoic Age is a term coined by Thomas Berry in the early 1980s as the current historical times in which he said we must come to terms with our relationship with the earth. Cited in: Thomas Berry, *The Great Work: Our Way into the Future.* New York: Broadway Books, 2000, p. 85. Ecozoic Age reference

A Letter from the Earth on the Call to Awakening

As I struggled for how to say this clearly for you all, I received a Letter from the Earth. She says it so well.

Dear One,

To awaken to life is your call.

I call not only you, but everyone, to awaken to the beauty, the bounty, the breadbasket of living to which you are born. Yes, I have created all of this for you, and for me, or so it seems, but I need for all of you to help me now.

The human species is spiraling out of control. You –– my intelligence, my pinnacle, my amazing glory – surprise and delight me with your ingenuity, but you became too focused on greed. And now I need you to stand back, stop, listen and make changes.

Please, Dear One, continue to awaken. Call others to awaken. As Thomas Berry wrote, this is your Great Work in this time – to speak up, to change the way you relate to the Earth. I will help you.

Be still. Be active. Be awake and answer my call.

Love, Gaia

My prayer is that this book will help you to awaken to the miraculous both within you and all around you and that it may spur you to action.

LEARNING TO SIMPLY SIT: MEDITATION

Dawn rises behind hollyhocks at Lakeside, Ohio, on Lake Erie

Learning to Sit

I am learning to sit.

Some days it's hard.

Some days it's easy.

I am learning to listen for God.

Some days I hear nothing.

Some days the love washes over me into joy.

I am learning that we are all connected.

Some days I still feel solitary.

Some days I realize that 10,000 others join me every moment.

I am opening to awareness deep within me.

Some days I feel empty.

Some days I feel that pulsating reality bringing life.

I keep thinking about the courage of the Hubble scientists.

Some days posed on emptiness in the sky.

Some days to realize the darkness contained infinite galaxies.

I keep thinking if I have the courage to sit in silence.

Some days I will focus on that emptiness, too.

Some days I will realize the web of stars and relationships hold us all.

Why Meditate?

The ancients practiced meditation to harmonize mind, body and spirit. Western Christianity often focuses on mind, a very cerebral approach to matters of the Spirit. But now many Christians are returning to the roots of their faith. Because God became flesh in Jesus, they argue that body is integral to the walk of those who follow Christ. Jesus offered Spirit, God's presence among his followers upon his departure. Many now seek to find the path toward integration of mind, body and spirit within the Christian tradition.

The scientists report that the human body works better with meditation. Meditation enhances the functioning of the brain. Meditation leads to unity consciousness, a sense of connection with people and all of creation. The brain, they tell us, comes wired for this experience of God. Those who meditate live longer. Health effects include lowering blood pressure, reducing heart disease, boosting the immune system and more.[7]

Did you know that Yoga was developed as a scientific approach to preparing the body for meditation? One Christian writer, Thomas Ryan,[8] who incorporates yoga

---

[7]Much scientific research continues to be conducted on the health benefits of meditation. Following are references to summaries of this research. See National Center for Complementary and Integrative Health at: nccih.nih.gov/health/meditation/overview and "Seven Ways Meditation can Change the Brain" by Alice Walton, *Forbes Magazine*, February. 9, 2015 and "14 Amazing Benefits of Meditation That Can Actually Rewire Your Brain" https://www.scienceofpeople.com/meditation-benefits/

[8]Thomas Ryan, *Prayer of Heart and Body: Meditation and Yoga as Christian Spiritual Practice.* Mahwah, New Jersey: Paulist Press 1995

and meditation into his prayer practice, notices that young people are often more interested in yoga studios than churches. But could this be their longing for a holistic spiritual approach?

Our materialistic society pulls us far away from the still, small voice of God. And yet, perhaps because our society clamors with so much urgency, so many images, so much stuff, we find ourselves drawn to leave the frenzy for the silence. The contemplative practice calls to us, leading us into the Center where our minds, bodies and spirits harmonize into the heart of God.

The Contemplative Gift of Simply Sitting

Contemplation is awakening to the presence of God in the human heart and in the universe, which is around us... knowledge by love. – Dom Bede Griffiths

Simply sitting into the presence of God provides a space of infinite growth and love. In this sacred place, one joins the Biblical pilgrims in the prayer of listening and being still before God. One connects with a deep wellspring of energy and inspiration for caring action. One cultivates harmony that leads to internal and external healing. And one becomes conscious of the unity of all beings, the earth and the cosmos.

Cultivating a meditation practices requires a daily commitment. A regular time and place for sitting meditation helps grow the contemplative's ability to enter the silence. At least 15 or 20 minutes daily is recommended for beginners.

There are a variety of ways to enter the silence. The Shalem Institute for Spiritual Formation recommends some form of body prayer to begin. Focusing on the breath, relaxation, a chant, a time of reading scripture or nature may be helpful. An infinite variety of entry points are possible. Whatever assists the pilgrim into that spacious silence of love should be followed. Experimenting with different tools may help the new contemplative find an effective practice.

The goal is to still the monkey mind and let

thoughts slip way. This, however, can be a difficult process. So be gentle with the self and the thoughts that come. Observing the thoughts that come and imagining them floating on down the river may be one way to let them go.

Those who have cultivated a path of contemplative practice report a journey that takes one through the dark night of the soul. Often, in early days, one finds a house-cleaning taking place. Entering the mystery provides a healing process. There are times of walking through the desert and other times of basking in the garden of delight.

Meditation provides many health benefits for the mind and body and helps tune the soul to Spirit. In addition, many people who maintain a regular practice find their lives unfold with less effort, less striving. Letting go into the presence of God's possibilities becomes increasingly commonplace in everyday life.

As the contemplative practice has grown in popularity, there are myriad resources available to assist those who seek this way. When the student is ready, the teacher arrives. So ask, knock, seek, and you will receive, the door will be opened, and you will find.

A Letter from the Earth on Learning to Sit

Water lily on Hope Lake, Hocking Hills, Ohio

Dear One,

When you sit in meditation, you fulfill all my desires for you. You stop. You listen. You merge your mind-body-spirit into the unity of my creation. You let go of thoughts which divide. You become one and experience the love at the center of life.

It's taken awhile for you to get it. I see you continuing to learn and struggle, even as you know it's so important for your well-being.

Nancy, I want to affirm your meditation practice. In fact, I'd like to challenge you to extend it into other parts of your day. Could you try a 15-minute meditation break at work? How about evening meditation with your husband?

I want you to live mindfully and to increase your ability to let go into the moment. You've tasted the goodness of silence and you've delved into the unity consciousness. If you can extend this into more of your day, you'll be surprised at the results and the simplicity that unfolds around you.

Learning to sit is quite a noble goal. Keep up the good efforts. Know I'm there, filling your life with joy and possibility. I love communing with you in this way.

Love, Gaia

Nancy's Thoughts on Learning to Sit

Meditation! What a gift! What a learning process! What a struggle! What a blessing!

When I wrote the poem, "Learning to Sit", I was just beginning my practice, eight years ago now. And today, I would say I'm still just beginning. Some people say we are all beginners when it comes to learning to sit.

If you're like me, you may resist the idea of sitting in meditation. I remember visiting a spiritual director as a young mother in my 30s. The director had Buddhist tendencies, even though she met me at a Catholic retreat center. She recommended that I incorporate silence into my spiritual practice. I remember laughing at the idea. Certainly, silence is something difficult to attain as a mother of young children. But, more than that, I just didn't see the value. I like to talk. I like to be busy. The practice of simply being did not appeal to me. Now I look back and wish I had taken her advice.

Some say that as we age, the appeal of "being" vs. "doing" grows! Certainly, as our bodies slow down, it's easier to sit and do nothing. Perhaps that is why I didn't begin my practice until I entered my 50s. But even then, it happened somewhat accidentally, a divine accident, I think, looking back.

I've always enjoyed spiritual learning. Throughout my life, I've enjoyed small groups and retreats, both as a participant and as a leader. One day, I discovered a learning opportunity online with the Shalem Institute for Spiritual Formation in Washington, D.C., to take a class in Leading Contemplative Small Groups and Retreats. Yes! Ever since I read Henri Nouwen in my 20s, I've loved the contemplative side of Christianity. So, I applied to take their 18-month course, not knowing that a requirement of the class would be to sit in silence every day for 20 minutes. After all those years, I began to mediate. Yes, it took me awhile to come to this practice.

Like most people who meditate, I found it difficult. At first, I expected instant enlightenment, sterling new insight, and deep inner peace. Actually, as I began, I learned that I shouldn't look for great insight, just letting go. And in reading *Interior Castles* by St. Teresa of Avila,[9] I learned that in order to get to the deep inner peace, you first must cross the moat. In her book, she uses the motif of the castle to describe the life of prayer. When she talks about the moat, she explains something that most meditators have discovered, that your stuff tends to surface when you work to become silent. The demons and dragons of your life return to disturb the waters of your practice. What also is true, though, is that as you let go of these demons and dragons, the pains of your life, you will find stiller waters, not only in your meditation time, but also in your daily life.

Many days, I still struggle with becoming silent. I readily admit that I am still a beginner after eight years of daily practice. And yet, I also know that this practice changed my life from inside out. Research shows

---

[9]Teresa of Avila (author) with Mirabai Starr (translator). *Interior Castle*. New York City, New York: Riverhead Books, 2004.

meditation calms the body and contributes to overall health. I've felt this benefit daily, as it calms me in early morning. When I do meditate later in the day, I'm amazed at how just a few minutes of concentrating on my breath and letting go of thoughts can transform my perspective. Suddenly, anxieties, worries, stress melt away. I know that Gaia's suggestion to do this during work breaks and in the evening is good advice.

The day I received this letter on simply sitting, I came home from work, stressed after working on several projects and seemingly nonstop activity. After dinner and watching TV, I contemplated drinking a beer, but instead went upstairs to sit with my husband and informed him that Gaia wants us to meditate together in the evening. He said he's willing, but he would probably go to sleep. I laughed and nodded.

He continued to work at his laptop, but the cat jumped up on my lap and I decided to go for it. I closed my eyes, slipping into silence, as my cat's purring led me into a relaxed state. Suddenly the anxieties of the day slipped away as goodness flowed through my veins and I settled into a time of meditation. Fifteen minutes later, I put the cat down and went downstairs to resume my evening activities. I no longer wanted a beer or to watch TV.

Once again, I see Gaia leading me into a better life. She explains simplicity will unfold around me if I meditate. She probably knows that I can complicate my life unnecessarily. Sometimes, for me, I've found life to be a struggle. But meditation reduces the struggle in a mysterious way.

Serendipities happen and life does unfold more easily after meditation. I've read about this, but I've also experienced it. I will express an intention to do something, and then as I walk through my day, the ducks line up to make it happen. People I need to help me show up unexpectedly. It's almost eerie sometimes, the way my day unfolds.

Here's an example that happened to me recently. Last year, I participated in a community garden, a wonderful project several miles from my house. My friends and I planted and watered and harvested our long plot all spring and summer. I loved the idea of participating, but I found it so difficult to find time before work to go water, to give up my Saturday mornings and to tend to my own garden at home. The chores competed with my morning meditation and writing time. Yet, as the signing time came this year, I signed up again. Then my friend said she didn't want to garden with me because I complained too much. This really felt painful, but also helped me realize that doing the garden was just too difficult for me. My husband again reminded me he couldn't understand why I ever took the project on in the first place. He knew I didn't have the time.

What to do? As I confronted my complaining self and knew I didn't really want a plot in the garden this year, I meditated one morning, and it came to me. What I really want to do is to support the garden project. When we filled out the paperwork, they asked for help with the common areas of flowers, around the exterior, to make it a beautiful place, with a new pollinator garden and with the big crops in community plots, such as potatoes and corn. I didn't sign up for that, because I knew just taking care of our plot would be too much. Now suddenly, I realized perhaps I could volunteer and support the garden project, learning more about gardening and not worrying about also tending a plot. I contacted the garden coordinator and told her I would serve as a supporter, rather than tending a personal plot. Answers for my life come more easily when I clear my mind in the morning.

Over time, I've come to understand that I'm encountering God as I meditate. In our scripture, there's a verse that we don't always know how to pray, but sighs intercede too great for words. That's what I think happens: I am just putting myself out there in God's presence and God stays with me through my day.

One of my friends shared once how hard it is to meditate. I suggested that maybe if she just reframed the practice as spending time with God, with the loving Spirit at the center of all life, it would not be so hard. She thanked me for that thought, saying that would help her.

Meditation is not for everyone. For some people who are recovering from trauma, such as racism, post-traumatic stress syndrome and domestic violence, the silence of meditation may be difficult and result in triggering repressed memories. In these situations, meditation would be more helpful if done within a counseling relationship. Or some may need to wait until after healing past trauma to begin a meditation practice. Still others find that that buried issues can be resolved in the silence.

Suggestions for Personal Practice of Meditation

1. Make a commitment to meditate every day and choose a time that works in your schedule. Try to dedicate 20 minutes, but if that is too difficult, start with 5 or 10 minutes to begin. Set a timer, so you don't have to focus on the clock. Most cell phones have a timer you can use.

2. Find a place in your home where you can be quiet and sit. Most suggest that you sit erectly, either cross-legged or with your feet flat on the floor. However, if that position does not work for you, honor your body and be comfortable. The goal is to be alert into the silence. You might need to ask the people in your life to honor your time in silence. If you have young children, it's probably easiest to meditate while they are sleeping.

3. Some people like to prepare an altar of sorts for sitting. I like to light a candle and have a vase of flowers with me, when possible. During the Christmas season, I love meditating in the dark with the Christmas tree lights twinkling and the glow of a candle. I usually meditate before dawn, but sometimes in the summer, when the days are longer and I rise later than usual, I also love meditating in the backyard with the flowers and plants. Breathing the fresh air, enjoying the oxygen of the trees and plants really

stimulates me in a deep way.

4. Spend some time experimenting with different strategies to see what works for you. Some suggest a mantra, repeating a word silently or out loud throughout the meditation time. I like to use the word "Shalom." I breathe in on the first syllable and out on the second. I like this because I breathe in with the "Shaaa" which is similar to the word for God in many languages (Yahweh, Allah, God). I imagine taking in the Ruah - the breath of God. And as I breathe out, I am holding the word "Om" which often is used as a way to tune into the energy of the universe. This helps me become one with all. The Jesus Prayer is another suggestion. "Lord have mercy on me, a sinner." Some suggest just focusing on your breath. I met a man once who just breathes slowly, counting as he breathes in to five and again as he breathes out. There are apps that can help you. I practice a variety of things myself.

5. Know that it may take you a long time to really learn to practice meditation, so be patient with yourself. Your goal is to let go of thoughts. Some like to imagine thoughts flowing past in a river. Don't fight your thoughts, just acknowledge them as part of you and then let them go. Using a mantra, focusing on the breath, counting are all strategies to occupy your mind to keep the

thoughts at bay.

6. If you have a devotional book, I find it's helpful to read a little before I go into silence. This week, I've been reading the *Wisdom of Thich Nhat Hanh* (2000). His experience as a meditator makes the reading helpful to me in my practice. Just a few paragraphs a day allows me to absorb the book slowly.

7. Try journaling after you meditate. In this way, you can capture insights that emerge from the silence. Silence tends to bring clarity. I find I do my best thinking after meditation. This time of journaling helps me prepare for whatever is coming up in my life. I also receive Letters from the Earth after I meditate! A good time to tune in to God for needed guidance.

8. You might try *Lectio Divina* with scripture or Nature to take you into the silence some days. See later chapters in this book for details.

An Experience of Simply Sitting with a Group

Introduction. Begin with a short introduction to sitting meditation and answer questions individuals may have. (5 minutes)

Body Prayer. Provide a time of gentle seated yoga stretches and breathing to heighten relaxation and awareness of the body. Lead into the time of silence, focusing on breath. (See next page for suggested script). (5 minutes)

Sitting Meditation. Provide a time of silence for meditation (20 minutes)

Journaling. Encourage journaling about the time of silence. (10 minutes)

1) How did the time of gentle yoga stretches and breathing assist or detract from your presence to your body and God?

2) Reflect on the quality of your meditation. To what extent were you able to let go into the silence of God's love?

3) Is this something that you would like to incorporate into your prayer discipline? Why or why not?

Sharing. Provide a time for people to discuss their experience of silent meditations and ask questions, share insights. (10 minutes)

Body Prayer: Seated Yoga Stretches

A suggested script for gentle seated yoga stretches and breathing to heighten relaxation and awareness of the body to lead into the time of silence, focusing on breath.

Get into a comfortable position, sitting up straight with both feet on the floor, or legs folded in a yoga position and close your eyes. Now take a deep breath in, counting 1-2-3-4-5 and then breathe out, counting back down. 5-4-3-2-1. Let's do this two more times. Breathe in 1-2-3-4-5 and out 5-4-3-2-1. And again, breathe in 1-2-3-4-5 and out 5-4-3-2-1. Okay, continue your breathing and counting as you stretch your arms slowly out to your sides and then up over your head, breathing in 1-2-3-4-5. Now breathe out, moving your arms slowly down, out to the sides and back to rest 5-4-3-2-1. And again... lift your arms up 1-2-3-4-5 and back down, 5-4-3-2-1. Now do a simple stretch, arching your back as you breathe in 1-2-3-4-5 and then rounding your back as you breathe out 5-4-3-2-1. And again, arch 1,2,3,4,5, and round 5-4-3-2-1. Now twist your torso to the right as you breathe in, placing your left hand on your right knee and your right hand behind you on the chair as you breathe in 1-2-3-4-5 and now as you breathe out, twist to the left, with your right hand on your left knee and your left hand behind on the chair 5-4-3-2-1. And again, breathe in and twist to the right 1-2-3-4-5. Breathe out and twist to the left 5-4-3-2-1. Now just sit silently and be aware of your body. How does it feel? Focus on your breath as it returns to its natural wisdom.

(Pause). When you're ready, open your eyes.

THE LABYRINTH WALK

A Wittenberg University student walks the Living Vine Labyrinth at Weaver Chapel

Sacred Path

At day's end,

> *I am often frazzled, depleted.*
>
> *They say the personality disintegrates*
>
> *in small children when they are tired.*
>
> *I, too, feel like this at times.*

At day's end,

> *Sometimes I walk the labyrinth.*
>
> *taking off my shoes, I slow down.*
>
> *I enter sacred space, enjoying soft music*

letting the path carry me.

The path winds

Around and back and forth, and I begin to unwind.

    My frazzled spirit dissolves as

    sweet loving presence caressing my soul.

I reach the center

    and know I am not alone.

    God is present there for me.

    I sit, kneel, or even lay flat on the cloth, resting in God.

    Dancing Spirit of Love, entwining with me.

When I rise, I long to dance.

    So, I twirl on the path out, dancing with God

    aware of love before and behind, moving within me.

    Preparing and then re-entering

    the dance of love in this everyday journey of mine.

Now I smile. I am at peace.

The Contemplative Gift of the Labyrinth

The labyrinth offers a wonderful gift for contemplative pilgrims. Movement in silence may enhance awareness of Spirit. This divine imprint provides a simple path to wind into the center and back out again. Ancient cultures utilized this archetype, dating back over 5,000 years. In the middle ages, Christians built labyrinths into the floors of cathedrals. Some believe they were used to imagine a pilgrimage to the holy land.

Nancy Finchbaugh with Lauren Artress at Ohio Labyrinth Workshop

Lauren Artress, an Episcopal priest, helped rebirth the modern labyrinth movement in recent years in the United States. With friends, she visited the labyrinth on the cathedral floor in Chartres, France. When she returned to her church in San Francisco, they created a similar labyrinth and she began teaching and leading workshops on the practice. Labyrinths can be found in churches, homes, and public places across the country.

The simple circular pattern of the labyrinth helps connect the walker with self and with God. The repetitive, symmetrical aspects of the path which wind around and back and forth tend to create balance and wholeness. Many report deep emotional and spiritual experiences when walking. Some also report a deep connection with the earth. Others experience a mysterious and mystical journey.

Some follow a practice of releasing, receiving, and returning. On the path to the center, they release and let go of any burdens or thoughts. In the center, they pause to receive a gift from God. On the journey out, they begin to return back into the world. Others like to ask a question before they walk, listening for answers on the way in, praying about the answers received in the center, and beginning to integrate the answers on the way back out. Artress offers a labyrinth workbook with varied purposes for the walk.

New walkers are encouraged to walk the labyrinth three times, before deciding whether or not to incorporate it into their spiritual practice. Veteran walkers often report each walk to be a unique experience.

A Letter from the Earth about Labyrinths

Nancy sitting in the center, Brookgreen Garden Labyrinth, S.C.

Dear One,

A labyrinth is a path to Me.

When you walk the labyrinth, you slow down, you enter silence. This is where you encounter my rhythm. There, in the center, you absorb the mystery of hope, of love, of joy.

You humans like to be busy, busy, busy. Running here, running there. Constant chattering on your devices and in your heads. The labyrinth, in contrast, lets you unwind.

The rhythmic pattern invites you to let go of the chatter, the busyness and your devices and simply move into the center. I want you to live from your center, with Me. That's what you find in the labyrinth.

Spiraling in and back out, you replicate a basic fractal in my created world – galaxies, roses, rain forest plants. You see that life emerges from the center of a seed, a bulb, even roots.

So it is with you, my friend, as you slow down and circle in with me, you will discover such a quality of life and love that will circle with you as you walk out.

It's a path of hope I walk with you.

Love, Gaia

Nancy's Thoughts on Labyrinths

As I read this letter from Gaia about labyrinths, I am reminded of the many times I have done just what She talks about here. So many times, the labyrinth helped me slow down, let go of thoughts and connect with both God and myself in a deeper way. Over the years of my labyrinth experiences, the labyrinth continues to teach me about walking in rhythm with life and living from my center. And each walk is different, always new, always comforting and enlightening at the same time. Such a gift these labyrinths offer to my life.

When I turned 50, my friends surprised me with a labyrinth mowed into the grass in a friend's backyard. For my first walk, I donned a red hat and purple boa and laughed. I enjoyed it, but I'm not sure I really got it. Later, one of these friends invited several of us to an indoors canvas labyrinth in a downtown church in a neighboring town. There, with soft music and lighted candles, I experienced more of what this sacred path can be, sensing the slowing and the prayer time of listening.

A few years later, when I enrolled in a class in leading contemplative small groups and retreats with the Shalem Institute, we were required to plan and lead a session on a contemplative practice, so I chose the labyrinth. I began to read and learn about labyrinths. I designed an experience for my small learning group at the retreat center where we met. We used an outdoor paved labyrinth for this session.

The next summer, when I helped my church plan a contemplative month for worship, I decided we should create our own labyrinth. In a two-week period, we designed and created what we call the "Living Vine Labyrinth," a canvas labyrinth that we have used for several years now, both in our church and in the community. You can read about our journey in the appendix (About the Living Vine Labyrinth)[10]. This labyrinth invited me deeper into a labyrinth journey.

We began to host monthly labyrinth walks at church. I became a "Certified Labyrinth Facilitator" with Lauren Artress' organization, Veriditas. Friends and I led labyrinth walks at a woman's reformatory, in the juvenile detention facility, for an urban neighborhood group, for a church women's retreat, at the local cancer center, and in the chapel at our local college.

As my concerns for our Earth have grown, I appreciate that the vines on our church labyrinth help me connect with the Earth as I walk. Later, I learned that labyrinth paths do put you into rhythm with the Earth as well, which Gaia also tells us.

There is a mystery about the labyrinth experience that I've witnessed both in my own life and while experiencing walks with others. Some call it a "thin" space, where the veil between heaven and earth seems lifted. There are times when I've heard from people who have passed on to the other side. Often, I have received wise counsel from God as I walk the questions of my life.

---

[10] See "About the Living Vine Labyrinth" by Nancy Flinchbaugh in "End Matters" of this book.

One of the most powerful experiences happened when a friend and I led a labyrinth walk at a women's prison. The spiritual energy in the room that day stayed with me through the coming week. One woman said she felt such love from the others in the silence, unlike the hostility she often experienced in the prison. The women wrote beautiful poems and thoughts afterward, explaining what the session elicited within them.

When we created the Living Vine Labyrinth, we placed flowers at each turn. They are the colors of the rainbow, and also the colors of the chakras, a new concept to me at the time. Now I really enjoy this aspect of our labyrinth, because it gives me a time to pray about my connection with God (crown chakra), my wisdom (third eye chakra), my voice (throat chakra), my heart (heart chakra), my fortitude (solar plexus), my creativity (womb chakra) and my roots (root chakra). I stop at the flowers with the various colors of these chakras that help my experience.

Lauren Artress told us in the training session I attended that she prefers cloth labyrinths because they seem to hold the Spirit, energy gathering from use over time. As strange as that seems, I think I've experienced it with our Living Vine Labyrinth. There's an incredible energy that fills the room and my heart when we set it up in our church fellowship hall, light candles, and turn on soft music. When we first started, we opened it once a month for a Friday happy hour. I later would say it is better than beer, because it would re-energize me after a frazzling work week.

Once, when a friend and I led a session at the local

juvenile detention center, I showed them a PowerPoint about the labyrinth and explained that they say that the labyrinth emerges in times of great chaos, so some people believe that's why it has come back into vogue today. I didn't think they'd get it. But they did. They understood that we are in a time of chaos, and they also really seemed to enjoy the walk, connecting in the center with each other.

So, I encourage you to try a labyrinth. You can probably find one in your community. Or maybe, like me, you'll decide to make your own!

Candlelit Living Vine Labyrinth at First Baptist Church, Springfield, Ohio

1. Read a book about labyrinths to learn more about walking them. A few that I find helpful are listed in the Bibliography at the end of this book. If you enjoy labyrinth-walking already, choose a book to learn about more ways to use a labyrinth. If you're new to labyrinths, choose an introductory book.

2. Check out the website "labyrinthlocator.org" to find labyrinths near you. You can also use this resource when traveling. Some labyrinths are in public places and churches, many quite accessible. Indoor labyrinths are usually open on a schedule.

3. Make a finger labyrinth to use. This can be as simple as finding a labyrinth image online and printing it out, and then playing the spiritual, jazz, drumming or classical music that resonates with you while tracing the path with your finger. If you have craft skills, you might want to carve one into wood, or add texture to the paper labyrinth to keep your finger in the lines. I recently learned to make a finger labyrinth on a 12-inch square canvas, covering the lines with thick twine or clothesline, then modge-podging it and finally painting it with acrylics. You can also buy a finger labyrinth. Check out the labyrinth resources websites for downloadable finger labyrinths, online labyrinths and places to buy them in the "Other Resources" section of "End Matters" of this book.

4. If you find an outdoor labyrinth near you, visit it on a regular basis and keep a journal of your experiences there. Watch the changing seasons.

5. You might want to make a labyrinth with a group or buy a labyrinth for personal use, many options abound. You can buy cloth labyrinths, kits with pavers for outdoor labyrinths, or you can be creative and make your own.

6. When you go on walks, you might just want to slip into silence and let it carry you. Other times, you

may ask a question and listen for answers as you walk. There are many ways to walk the labyrinth. Some people prefer music for labyrinth walks, and others prefer silence. Labyrinth facilitators recommend using instrumental music without associated words. But experiment with the music that takes you to spiritual space within your own or others' traditions. Native American flute music, classical guitar, or lively New Orleans jazz may contribute to your labyrinth walk, as may African-American gospel music, instrumental hymns or drumming.

An Experience of Labyrinth Walking for a Group

Labyrinth Retreat at First Baptist Church, Springfield, Ohio

Introduction. Begin with an introduction to labyrinth as contemplative practice, including instructions for walking (5 minutes).

Body Prayer. Lead the group in a guided meditation, focusing on the gift of hands and feet. See next page for a suggested script (5 minutes).

Silence. Provide a time of silence for the group to walk the labyrinth. If there are many people, divide into two groups and have some try a finger labyrinth, while others walk the labyrinth and then switch halfway through. Instrumental music helps many while walking the labyrinth, but some might prefer silence. Talk about this before you begin. This time may need to be longer, based on the size of the group and the labyrinth (25 minutes).

Reflection. Ask the group to reflect and/or journal on the following:

1. How was your experience of the time of body prayer, focusing on your hands and feet? How did that help/not help your awareness of God?

2. What was your experience of walking the labyrinth with your feet and/or fingers?

3. Do you want to include labyrinth walking in your spiritual practice? Why or why not?

Group Sharing. Provide time for the group to share observations, experiences. Close with a prayer of thanksgiving. Perhaps go around the circle and give each person a chance to share a sentence of thanksgiving for this time. (10 minutes)

Body Prayer: Self-Massage of Hands and Feet

A suggested script for massaging the hands and feet to heighten relaxation and awareness of the body, leading into a time of labyrinth walking.

To prepare for this meditation, ask people to remove their shoes and, if it's warm enough, also their socks. Explain: In this meditation, we are going to gently massage our hands and our feet. This is a nice practice that you can do to help you relax. Those who practice reflexology would say it's also a form of self-healing. There are points on both the hands and the feet that correspond to various parts of your body. When you massage places with tension, it helps let that tension go in corresponding body parts as well.

So, first, let's give God thanks for our hands. *(Do these steps yourself to model the self-massage as you explain the steps).* Use your right hand to massage your left hand. Use your thumb to make small circles on your palm and then, using your thumb on top and forefinger underneath, massage each finger from the place it connects with your hand, out to the tip. Also massage the area between the thumb and the forefinger. This is a good place to massage when you have a headache. Turn your hand over and continue the process on the other side of the hand and massage the fingers again, and as you do, express gratitude for the many ways your hands and fingers help you each day. Marvel at the miracle of your hand.

Now, repeat this process on your right hand, using your left hand to first massage the palm and the fingers, then turn your hand over and do the other side. *(Give people time to complete the process on the second hand. When they have completed the process, ask them to cross their right foot over their left knee. If they are unable to do this, suggest they get in another position to reach their right foot with their hand, or they can again massage their hand instead.)*

Now we are going to massage our feet, again giving thanks for them as they serve us. Begin, as you did with your hand, only using both hands, use your thumbs to massage the bottom of your foot, cradling your foot with your fingers, and then massage each toe from where it joins the foot out to the nail. Then repeat the action again with the top of your foot, massaging with your thumb and then your thumb and forefingers on your toes. Consider all the places your feet take you and how they help you each day to live your life. Also massage the sides of your feet, using whichever fingers work for you.

Now put your right foot down and cross your left foot over your right knee and repeat the process. Massage the bottom of your foot, through the arch and around the pads of the ankle and up by the toes. Massage each toe… *(Give them time to complete this)* Then the tops of your feet, the toes again. And the sides of your foot. Finish up and, as you return to a resting pose, consider how your body feels after this loving attention.

Close with a short prayer: Loving God, we give you thanks for the gift of our hands and feet that make our lives so much easier. Help us to remember to take care of our hands and feet and to share love with them each day. We pray in the name of Jesus. Amen.

SACRED CONVERSATION

"Listening is a form of spiritual hospitality by which you invite strangers to become friends, to get to know their inner selves more fully, and even dare to be silent with you." – Henri Nouwen

Listening

You listen.

I speak.

You acknowledge me.

I smile.

You hear me.

I tell you more.

You validate my journey.

I laugh.

Your presence

Becomes Spirit

Sitting with me and

I thrive.

Sacred Conversations/Holy Listening

Contemplative practice brings an oasis of solitude into the busy world in which we dwell. Gradually, we learn the value of slowing down to reflect, restore, and listen for God. While we cultivate individual practices, we also need spiritual companionship to guide and journey with us. It's crucial to find and create space for sacred conversation and holy listening.

Throughout time, religious communities created space for conversation and listening. Jesus created a small group, calling 12 disciples as he began his ministry. This circle became a community that listened and learned together. Monastic communities have long practiced one-on-one conversations to teach and instruct newcomers. Pastoral counseling developed within the church to provide a place for listening. In many spiritual traditions, there are gurus who teach and instruct in the practice of meditation.

Today, the contemplative community encourages distinctive listening practices to support those who journey into silence. Spiritual Directors are trained to listen to a person one-on-one and meet monthly to help a person discuss and consider their faith journey. James Keegan, SJ explains this process as "Spiritual direction is the contemplative practice of helping another person or group to awaken to the mystery called God in all of life, and to respond to that discovery in a growing relationship of freedom and commitment."[11]

A Spiritual Friendship performs a similar function, where mutual listening assists both persons. Yet another approach involves small listening groups, where several people sit together and listen to each other, one by one. A variation of this process is a Spiritual Direction group, where the group intentionally functions as a spiritual director for each member.

We all need someone to listen to us. To be heard without judgment can be transformative. When we listen for God together, we find light shining into sorrows, we find hope and validation along our way. We voice our truth and live into new paths of hope.

---

[11] James Keegan, S.J. Reference: https://www.sdiworld.org/find-a-spiritual-director/what-is-spiritual-direction.

A Letter from the Earth on Sacred Conversation and Holy Listening

Dear One,

Thank you for making space in your life for sacred conversation. When you listen to your friends in your Shalem Circle, when you meet with your spiritual director, you are listening for Me in new ways.

It's so important for each person to be heard. In the process of listening with each other for God in your lives, you identify the Spirit moving in and among you. You find companions on your spiritual journey.

You are the way I communicate. When you listen with compassion, you become my heart beating for the person we both love. When others listen to you, you feel my love extending hope, joy, validation, and deep caring into your life.

So, Dear One, cultivate these sacred conversations, not just on Skype and Google Hangout, but in your church community. These are the powerful conversations which will bring change to our world.

Study the process. Encourage your faith community to practice listening. Be creative in making more space in your life for sacred conversation. This is what I want for you all.

Love, Gaia

Nancy's Thoughts on Sacred Conversation and Holy Listening

Shalem Circle Friends Liz Kuhn and Anita Davidson with me at Lakeside and in Columbus

Don't you love Gaia's take on things? Do her words resound into your heart the way they do mine? I so love this guidance she pours into my life. I know it's directed to me, but I think it can also be beneficial to you and she tells me to share them with you.

Her words, "You are the way I communicate," startles me into the truth about sacred conversations in a very deep way. "You can be my heart beating for the person we both love." She underscores the importance of both listening and being heard in this beautiful love letter.

Throughout my life, I've been blessed with good listeners. I remember a time in particular when I became very confused on my spiritual journey. I once heard that a thinking Christian struggles at least every seven years with their faith and belief in God. Perhaps, our image of God becomes too small for the reality of the One who created us all. For me, this happened in young adulthood as I tried to resolve the many variations of theology I learned in college. I left the church for a while. One night, someone listened to me. He didn't judge me but acknowledged the difficulty of my journey and my unanswered questions. I still remember his compassion that became a bridge into a deeper faith journey for me.

Now I have a spiritual director who I meet with regularly. She helps me consider how God is moving in my life. She listens to my struggles, encourages me along the way and validates the way God is guiding and speaking in my life. I value her presence and listening

Loretta Farmer, Spiritual Director

My Spiritual Director Listens to Me on Skype

with me. For example, you've been reading my Letters from the Earth in this book. I talk to her about the letters I receive. She encourages me to continue to listen, and she affirms the messages I hear. She wants me to share these messages. At times, I worry that people will think I'm totally bonkers, but she assures me that these are good messages and they need to be heard. "Who else will speak for the Earth?" she asks me.

Spiritual directors are not therapists or counselors, but instead, they help a person explore a deeper relationship with the spiritual aspect of being human. They help people tell their sacred stories. Spiritual direction helps us learn how to live in peace, with compassion, promoting justice, as humble servants of that which lies beyond all names.

In this letter, Gaia affirms that we each need to listen, but also be heard, and she affirms the ways I'm already doing this. When I finished my program with Shalem, I was encouraged to join a Shalem Circle, to meet monthly with a circle to listen and support our contemplative leadership. For the past seven years now, I've been blessed to be a part of a small group that meets to listen and encourage one another along the way. We usually meet in person or by Google Hangout. We do not give each other advice, but listen for God as we listen to each other, sharing and then praying for each other.

Throughout my life, I've treasured small group experiences which help me feel a sense of companionship and prayer support on my journey. You notice that Gaia suggests I need to encourage more of this within my own church? Right now, both my spiritual director and Shalem Circle live in Columbus, about an hour away. Gaia wants me to foster such contemplative connections here in my own community as well. One thing I love about her letters is that she always points me in good directions. I'm not sure exactly how I'll try to do what she asks, but I know I will work on this.

Contemplative small groups are different than other small groups of which I've been a part. Here, after check-ins, sharing what's up with us recently, we take time to listen to each of us fully. We share whatever is trending for us in our lives. Yesterday, I met with my Shalem Circle. One person shared about her grief journey, another shared about the way she's finding silence in her life during this time. I shared about my life mission, which is to serve God and people and to work for peace, social justice and the Earth. I wonder now if it still works. After I shared, we had a time of silence and listening together for God. Then my friends shared their response to my sharing. One said that they heard me not wondering if the "what" of my mission needs to be changed, but considering the "how" of living out my mission in this time. They both affirmed me in my mission work. I came away feeling good about my life mission and also committed to continue to listen to how I can best live that out in these days of my life.

As I've experienced the transformative power of being heard in my own life and heard stories of how listening transforms others, I've made a commitment to do more listening. Recently at a Shalem Gathering, a new friend explained a process in San Francisco, where her community listens to street people. They set up two chairs on the sidewalk with a sign announcing "When you talk, we listen." Then they sit, waiting for whoever needs to be heard on a given day. I also know of a program in Columbus called "Women-to-Women"[12] for low income women, single mothers, and those facing a myriad of issues, such as re-entering society from prison and overcoming drug and alcohol problems. Their approach is to listen, as well.

For several years, I've been a part of another type of listening circle, initiated by a local program called "Circles." At the time, two national non-profits (Move the Mountain and Bridges out of Poverty) partnered in a project to help people move out of poverty. An important part of the program involved small groups of "Circle Leaders" who were navigating their way out of poverty, and "Allies" who were there to support and provide networking connections. When my Circle met, we listened to each other, shared our personal goals and related progress and prayed for one another. This group continues to be important to us all as we navigate our lives and work to reach our goals. Over time one of our Circle members paid off her debt, bought a house and completed college.

When seeking a spiritual director, friend or listening circle, finding someone who resonates with your experience and faith journey is so important. You may need to search for awhile until you find someone or a group that is good for you. Many of the spiritual directors come from the white "European" Christian traditions. A person of color and/or oppressed minority may find a need for a person from their own ethnic

---

[12] Women-to-Women, Columbus Spirituality Network. Reference: https://spiritualitynetwork.org/women-to-women.

background, who talks the language of their experience and oppression.

Several years ago, Therese Taylor-Stinson founded an organization, the Spiritual Directors of Color Network. Together, they have crafted books that explore the needs and approaches to help in spiritual guidance with people who have suffered discrimination and oppression both historically and in their personal lives. See Bibliography: *Embodied Spirits: Stories of Spiritual Directors of Color* (2013), *Ain't Gonna Let Nobody Turn Me Around: Stories of Contemplation and Justice* (2017) and *Kaleidoscope Broadening the Palette in the Art of Spiritual Direction* (2019). They are doing good work, so important for all spiritual directors as they seek to be responsive to their directees.

With the availability of video chats now, it's easy to connect with people in different parts of the country, even if no one is available locally. I've Skyped with my spiritual director for several years and find it rewarding and better than a long commute. The websites of both Spiritual Directors International (sdi.com) and Spiritual Directors of Color Network (sdc.com) provide directories of spiritual directors. You can also contact local religious organizations for referrals.

I know that Gaia is so right in asserting the need for the contemplative space of listening.

Suggestions for Personal Practice

1. If you don't already have a spiritual director, I recommend you try this approach for a year. A spiritual director is trained to listen to you and guide you in your spiritual life. They go through a training program which teaches them how to be good listeners and companions on the spiritual journey. Usually, you meet once a month for an hour and pay them for their service. Some have sliding scales and encourage you to pay what you can afford, others have a set rate. Most large cities have a cadre of spiritual directors. Inquire at local churches until you find options. With internet video chatting options, even if you live in a remote area, you can meet with someone online. My spiritual director lives an hour away. I used to go visit her, but now we almost always meet by Skype, which saves me two hours of driving. You should consider interviewing or meeting with several possible directors and then choose the one that seems right for you in your journey.

2. An additional one-on-one option would be to enter into a spiritual friendship. Rather than meeting with a trained spiritual director, you can be good listeners for each other. Invite a church friend or close companion to consider doing this with you. If they agree, set a regular schedule to meet and listen to each

other and pray for each other. It's helpful to have a format you follow, and to agree to the length of time you'll meet. There are books written about this that may help guide you. A simple approach would be to start with silence, then have a time for each of you to share, followed by a time of listening for God, sharing any insights and then praying for the person who shared, and then repeat the process for the other person. You might meet weekly, every two weeks, or monthly. Find a rhythm that works for you.

3. Rather than enter into a long-term relationship, you might also look for opportunities to incorporate listening into classes and other times. Perhaps, consider this approach when you get together with a friend you haven't seen for a while. I like to plan for times of one-on-one sharing during discussions in Sunday School classes. This gives a chance for individuals to be heard and to listen to another, which I think often deepens the experience in the class.

An Experience of Contemplative Listening for a Group

Silent Retreat Gathering at St. Mary's, Columbus, Ohio

Introduction. Begin with an introduction to contemplative listening. (5 minutes)

Body Prayer. Namaste Greetings. Namaste means "The Spirit in me bows to the Spirit in You." Explain this and demonstrate the Namaste bow. Have the group stand, in a circle. Start by standing in front of the person to your left, bowing and saying Namaste. Instruct them to bow back, also repeating Namaste. Move on to the next person. Have each person follow you around the circle, so when you finish, all in your group will have bowed to each other. (5 minutes, or longer, depending on the size of the group.)

Silence. Introduce a time of silence. (5 minutes)

Personal Sharing. Begin a time for personal sharing. Ask each person to limit their sharing to 5 minutes or longer, depending on how long you have for the activity. For each person, follow this approach:

1. One person shares

2. 2 minutes of silence for listening

3. Group sharing, affirming their situation, sharing how they heard God speaking.

4. Ask how they would like the group to pray for them.

5. 1 minute of silent prayer

6. Next person shares.

Silent Writing/Drawing. Continue with a time of silent writing, doodling and/or drawing reflecting on the time. Instrumental music may be played in the background. (10 minutes)

Reflection. Reflect and/or journal on the following:

1. How was your experience of the time of the namaste prayer? In what ways did that help or not help your awareness of God within each of the persons gathered?

2. What was your experience of sharing and being heard during this time? In what ways was this helpful to you? Were there any problems for you in sharing in this way?

3. How was your time of listening to the others? Did you hear God speaking?

4. How did the times of silence help or hinder your

ability to be present to God and each other?

5. How did the time of journaling and/or drawing assist in your contemplative experience of sacred conversation?

Group Sharing. Provide time for the group to share observations, experiences. Then close with a prayer of thanksgiving. Perhaps go around the circle and give each person a chance to share a sentence of thanksgiving for this time.

GRATITUDE PRACTICE

Welcoming Day, Surfside Beach, S.C.

Choosing Delight

Every morning I begin my day in silence.

Often before the sunrise,

I sit in prayer

encountering God in the sacred space of now.

Then, I open my journal

to ruminate

and always, I begin with thanksgiving, --

choosing to cultivate delight.

A very simple discipline --

focusing on fullness,

naming silver and gold --

treasures buried deep within each breath.

My body shifts into smile.

My spirit lifts into joy.

My mind dwells in possibilities of

abundant harmony, holy delight.

The Contemplative Gift of Gratitude

"If the only prayer you say in your life is "thank you," that would suffice."--Meister Eckhart

Cultivating a spirit of gratitude transforms life into an experience of grace. By giving thanks, one focuses the mind on the positive aspect, thereby creating positive energy of spirit and health in the body.

The people of the Bible include this practice in their life of prayers. The worship book of the Hebrews (Psalms) brims with gratitude. The Psalmist recommends: "Sing to the Lord with thanksgiving; sing praises on the harp to our God." (Psalm 147:7). When Jesus heals the 10 lepers, only one returns to give thanks. He tells the grateful Samaritan that his faith has made him well (Luke 17). The epistles include instructions to give thanks. "Be anxious for nothing, but in everything by prayer and supplication, with thanksgiving, let your requests be made known to God." (Philippians 4:6). Also in Thessalonians 5:18, we read: "In everything give thanks; for this is the will of God in Christ Jesus for you."

In contemplative practice, gratitude can be both an entry point and the fruit of faithful discipline. A time of silence can begin with a prayer of thanksgiving. "Thank You" can serve as a mantra during meditation. Rather than fighting the thoughts that come, this mantra offers an expression of thanks for each thought, before letting it go. Journaling, doodling, and drawing thanks can also be a form of contemplative gratitude. This might take the form of writing a poem or prayer of thanksgiving, drawing symbols of blessings, and/or making a list of events, people, and things for which one is grateful. And then within the spaciousness of God's love, the fruit of joy and gratitude will begin to permeate the life of the dedicated practitioner.

Recent scientific discoveries within quantum physics suggest the observer influences what happens. Our outlook on life transforms not only our inner world, but also events and people around us. When we choose gratitude as a daily practice, we cultivate joy for ourselves and others.

A Letter from the Earth on Gratitude

Field of Gratitude, Tecumseh Land Trust Sunflowers, Yellow Springs, Ohio

Dear One,

When you say thank you, you sense me in all my glory. You tap into the reality of your life as blessing and joy. That is why I call you to live in an awareness of gratitude. Because then you dwell in the miracle of life and believe me... You are a miracle.

You humans take life for granted and get hung up in so much that doesn't really matter in the scheme of things. Your almighty Dollar. Progress. Politics.

I created you for more than that. That is why I call you to dance. I want you to live your days with happy abandon. I want you to love and laugh.

You have a choice. Those Kaufmans* got it right. When faced with difficulties, you can give in to despair or you can choose *happiness, gratitude and joy.*

Give thanks. Find that silver lining. Dance with the fairies who are rolling out a red carpet into your day even as we speak.

And Dear One? Thank you for listening.

Love, Gaia.

*Neil Barry Kaufman wrote *Happiness is a Choice* which I discuss below.

Nancy's Thoughts on Gratitude

As I read over the Earth's letter on gratitude, I remember how gratitude changes me and brings me much joy. I listen to Meister Eckhart's words… "If the only prayer you say in your entire life is 'Thanks', it will suffice." Gratitude is an attitude. All so true.

As a human, it is very easy to dwell on the frustrations in life. Believe me, I do. I can be very good at that. But I also work at drawing close to God, and I look for spiritual practices that help me grow. I believe gratitude to be one of those practices.

For many years now, I start my morning pages of journaling each day by listing five things for which I'm thankful. I almost always start by giving thanks for a new day. It's a small thing, but I am really thankful for the gift of another day of life, and especially a time of morning reflection where I meditate, journal, write, and pray. Life shines with such a sacred quality in this early hour. I go on to remember special moments, people, learnings, events, answers to prayer from my previous day. Such a gift to start my day with these smiles.

In my young life, my friends and I became enamored with a book called *Power in Praise* by Merlin Carothers (1980). As a Christian, the Bible tells me to "give thanks in all circumstances," 2 Thessalonians 5:17. Carothers elaborates on that approach and suggests that there is something transformative that happens when you choose to give thanks, even for those situations that seems so bad.

Cancer? I remember an older friend, a woman in my

church, who was diagnosed with stomach cancer at 88. She asked me, "Nancy, is it wrong to say that I'm thankful for cancer? If I never got this illness, I would never have known how people feel about me."

Why was she so happy? Because our pastor told us in church one Sunday that she was lonely and we should visit her. I did. As I sat with her, I had an idea. I decided to make an appreciation book for her. It's a little project I've done quite a few times for people when they are sick, or in transition, celebrating a birthday or graduation, or retiring. I ask friends and family to fill out a sheet and return it to me, filling in the blank for several prompts. "What I appreciate about you is…", "Thank you for…", "My prayer for you is…", "A special memory I have with you is..." I then type these into a computer and print them out on photo size sheets and also ask for photos of the people who are sharing. I combine these into little photo albums for the person. I made one of these for this woman, and suddenly, she knew that the people in her church truly appreciated her smile, her kind words, her presence with us each Sunday. She kept it by her bedside, reading it again and again. "If I didn't get sick, I never would have known how they felt about me, Nancy," she told me.

It's one of the mysteries of the contemplative life that ripples of goodness extend out from one life into another when we take time to express appreciation and thanks. If you'd like to try this project, I have directions in the appendix for how you can do it. It helps that I'm a photo hound, so I often already have quite a few photos I can use of people in my church and life.

Another way I practice gratitude is on Thanksgiving each year. Instead of writing a list of five things, I challenge myself to go to 100. The first time I did this, I noticed my whole body felt lighter and happier that day. As gratitude shifts the inner self to joy, it affects not only the mind and spirit, but also our physical selves. Such a very good way to live.

These days, there are so many books written on this topic. I think Sarah Ban Breathnach's book on *Simple Abundance* (1997) inspired me to incorporate thanksgiving into my morning pages. Her recommendation is to start a gratitude journal, but since I already journaled every day, I decided I could just add it to my practice. Another book I found transformative is by Barry Neil Kaufman, *Happiness is a Choice* (1994). When Barry and his wife gave birth to a severely disabled child, they were instructed to put the child into an institution. But they chose to ignore that advice and to choose happiness, welcoming the child as a gift which became transformative for them, eventually writing about it to share their story of joy.

My mother on Easter, five years after her terminal diagnosis, 2006

I gave this book to my mother in her later years after I read it. A month later, she learned her breast cancer had spread to her tailbone. I didn't think she had time to read the book, and I never would have given it to her after her diagnosis. But in fact, she did read it and proceeded to write a letter to me and other close family members, asserting that she was choosing happiness in the time she had left. She instructed us to help her laugh when we came to visit, rather than to cry. So when we visited, my sons would read her jokes. We played games and laughed. We watched funny movies and tv shows. And my mother's cancer disappeared. I know that doesn't always happen, but there is a book about that, too… *Anatomy of an Illness* by Norman Cousins (2001) who laughed his way back to health. "Laughter is the best medicine," they say. What a gift to me, so liberating, that my job in visiting my mom during her illness was to help her laugh. So contagious. We all had a good time.

My writing coach, Kathie Giorgio, experienced several whammies in recent years, including an assault while walking her dogs by a man wearing a "Make America Great Again" hat in the week after the presidential election. Not wanting to give in to despair, she made a commitment to blog each day about one thing for which she was grateful in the midst of very difficult times. She called it "Today's Moment of Happiness Despite the News." Shortly thereafter, she received a diagnosis of Stage 2 breast cancer, and then her husband lost his job, taking with it her health insurance. The blog became quite popular and her publisher turned it into a book, *Today's Moment of Happiness Despite the News* (2019). She says now that this practice saved her life.

Just yesterday, I led our adult forum at church, contemplating the end of another year. As we sat in a circle, sharing, a friend on disability income shared her overflowing gratitude for God, the children, youth and her church family. I once again was reminded that it's not so much how much we have materially that leads us to a focus on gratitude, but how we choose to respond to the life we live.

I encourage you to find a way to make gratitude a daily practice. And I believe you will find, like so many others, that it will truly change your life.

Nancy's Gratitude Lists

Typical Day – List of Five 2/23/19

Modeling my new hoodie with my husband, Steve

1. Thank you for a new day.

2. Thank you for the weekend and a Saturday at home

3. Thank you for the sweatshirt Steve gave me for Valentine's Day, a pink hoodie from the Ellen Store that says "Be Kind to One Another" that keeps me warm on this winter morning.

4. Thank you for the Turmeric-Ginger-Echinacea tea I found at the grocery store yesterday and am enjoying this morning

5. Thank you for the idea of fractals in the book,

Emergent Strategy, that I'm reading, a new idea of how to focus on intentionality in small groups, organizing, being the change you wish to see.

My 2018 Thanksgiving Gratitude List "100" – 11/22/2018

1. Family

2. Meals

3. Saturday

4. Wednesday Night (We had a dinner party with the following people:

5. Bre Tree

6. Tiffany Cydrus-Beckel

7. Robert Beckel

8. Getting our car fixed.

9. Steve (husband)

10. Jacob (son)

11. Luke (son)

12. Luke's girlfriend

13. Thanksgiving

14. Hope

15. Letters I receive from the Earth

16. Rev. Ken Whitt (former pastor)

17. Ken Whitt's book on the science and spirituality he's working on and I've been reading to offer comment

18. First Baptist Church (my church)

19. Rev. Adam Banks (our pastor)

20. My spiritual director – Loretta Farmer

21. Tiffany Wanzo

22. Going to Seattle in two weeks!

23. Finishing writing my third novel,

Revelation in the Roots.

24. Lori Whitaker

25. Thanksgiving Playlist – music

26. Music

27. Shannon Meadows (my boss)

28. Neighborhood facilitation project at work

29. Book launch for *Letters from the Earth* in October

30. Everyday Democracy

31. New novel I'm writing (*Revelation on the Sea Island*)

32. *Learning to Sit* book project

33. Four days off for Thanksgiving

34. Feeling Happy

35. A New Day

36. Friendship with old work partner – Mike Crockett

37. People at church

38. FBC Women's Retreat we had two weeks ago

39. Shalem Institute for Spiritual Formation

40. Writing career

41. Kathie Giorgio (writing coach)

42. My brother, Paul Flinchbaugh, and his wife, Angela

43. Photos on Facebook

44. Extended Family

45. Cousin Lynne Johnson

46. Peg and Ian Reese housing Jacob in Pasadena last summer

47. Jacob (son) visiting from LA for Thanksgiving

48. My life

49. Steve's upcoming knee replacement surgery

50. Visiting niece and her husband – Anne Flinchbaugh and Tom Baniasak in Seattle soon.

51. Gardening

52. Mom's Plant (Peace Rose in corner, given to me when my mom died 12 years ago)

53. Time with my sister-in-law, Mary Fontana in October in Dallas

54. That she can be with Tom's family in Chicago for Thanksgiving

55. Other plants

56. Winkie Mitchell

57. Christmas cactus blooming at work

58. Blooms

59. Holidays

60. Cousin Dottie Turner coming for Christmas

61. Friend Barb Whitmore coming at Christmas

62. The violin

63. Entertaining

64. Coffee

65. Cinnamon in coffee

66. Caffeine rush

67. Delightful body

68. Back laying technique for sciatica pain relief

69. Jacob healing

70. Conversation with Jacob

71. Photography

72. My contemplative life

73. Foot rubs

74. Massages

75. Traveling

76. Going to LA in February to visit Jacob!

77. Floating on air

78. Naureen Qasim

79. Steve cooking Thanksgiving meal and many others.

80. Steve doing laundry.

81. Steve retired.

82. Connections

83. My clothes

84. iPad

85. Our house

86. Candles

87. Heaters

88. Healing body

89. Maria Soto

90. The plant growing under the lamp

91. Meaningful life path

92. Labyrinth

93. Living Vine

Labyrinth

94. My creative life

95. Mom and Dad

96. Aunt Ginger
and Uncle Don

97. Uncle Bob

98. The cello

99. Christmas
Music

100.   This list!

Suggestions for a Personal Gratitude Practice

1) Pick a time each day to give thanks. If you already have a journaling practice, incorporate that into your journal. If not, consider keeping a small notebook by your bed and make a list of five things from the day for which you are grateful, every night before you go to bed. Or if you prefer, do it when you first wake up. Take time once a week, perhaps on Sunday, to read over the gifts of your week.

2) Take time to give thanks for the food before you eat. Consider not only a general note of thanks, but for the gifts and miracle of the Earth, for those who harvested, for the animals who gave their lives, for all the workers who labored to get this food to your table, and also give thanks for the ways the food will nourish your body and give you energy for your day.

3) Make a habit of writing thank you notes and appreciating the people in your life.

4) Consider making an appreciation book for someone going through a transition, celebrating a milestone, or facing a major illness. Read suggestions on how to make this book in the appendix.

5) Use "You, I thank" as a meditation mantra. As you breathe in, say or think, "You," picturing God or your higher power, the Spirit of life, being aware of how this breath sustains and gives you life. As you breathe out, say or think, "I thank." Continue with this rhythm throughout your meditation, or at least for 10 repetitions before you slip into silence.

6) Create art to express your gratitude. This could be a photograph, a musical composition, a sketch or

painting, or a poem or longer piece of writing.

7) If you like to post to social media, experiment with gratitude posts. Post a photo, giving thanks for an event, a person, nature, etc. This will brighten another person's day as they see your joy on Facebook, Instagram, Twitter. Practicing gratitude sends ripples of happiness.

8) Experiment with other ways of expressing and focusing on gratitude. You may find a better way that emerges from your own life. If you do, let me know what other practices you've designed. Email your ideas to me at nancy.flinchbaugh@gmail.com.

An Experience of Contemplative Gratitude for a Group

Introduction. Begin with an introduction to gratitude as contemplative practice (5 minutes)

Body Prayer. Lead the group in a guided body prayer of gratitude. In the prayer, ask them to focus on many body features one at a time, from head to feet, including eyes, nose, mouth, ears, brain, throat, skeletal system, circulatory system, digestive system, etc. First ask them to consider how the body part functions to assist their life and then ask them to thank that body part for its service, and to also thank God for the miracle of its work in their body. See the next page for script you can use for this prayer. (5 minutes)

Silence. Introduce a time of silence, using "Thank You" as a mantra (10 minutes)

Silent Writing/Drawing. Continue with a time of silent writing, doodling and/or drawing your thanks. Instrumental music may be played in the background. (10 minutes)

Reflection. Reflect and/or journal on the following:

1. How was your experience of the time of body prayer, focusing on gratitude for your body? In what ways did that help or not help your awareness of God?

2. What was your experience of sitting in silence, using "thank you" as your mantra? Any resistances? Challenges?

3. How did the time of journaling and/or drawing assist in your contemplative experience of gratitude?

Group Sharing. Provide time for the group to share observations, experiences. Then close with a prayer of thanksgiving. Perhaps go around the circle and give each person a chance to share a sentence of thanksgiving for this time.

Body Prayer: Guided Meditation on Gratitude for the Body

A suggested script for a guided meditation of thanksgiving for the miracle of the human body to heighten relaxation and awareness of the body, leading into a time of gratitude.

Get in a comfortable position, sitting, or lying down. Close your eyes and take a deep breath and let it out. I'm going to guide you in a prayer of thanksgiving for your body. First, let's thank God for our heads. Place your hands on the top of your head. Give thanks for your hair, your skull, your brain. Take a moment to marvel at the miracle of this part of your body. Now explore your face with your hands. Thank God for your eyes that give you sight. For your nose, which helps you enjoy your food and enables you to breathe. Take a breath in through your nose, let it back out, and thank the nose for its service. Now consider your mouth. Smile. Thank it for its help in expressing emotion. Thank it for the mouth's help in breathing. Take a deep breath in through your mouth and let it out, then acknowledge its service. Consider and give thanks for your teeth and tongue and their help with eating and preparing food for the digestive process. And then consider your throat and vocal chords therein. Thank all of it for helping you speak. Consider the esophagus, taking food down to your stomach. Be amazed and grateful for this process. Now consider your ribs and lungs and take another deep breath, feeling them serving you as you breathe. Give thanks for them. And place your hands on your heart. Feel its gentle beat and imagine the way it helps circulate blood throughout your body, endlessly pumping in such a miraculous way, making your life possible. Move on down through your abdomen and give thanks for your stomach, your intestines, your sexual organs. Now consider your arms, your hands, your legs and your feet. Give thanks for all of them and the way they help you live your life. Take a moment now to just rest in your body and consider how it functions as a whole. Be grateful for the miracle of life you are. Closing prayer: "Oh God, as we consider the miraculous aspects of our body, we give thanks to you. We can barely comprehend this mystery of life, constantly supporting us every moment of our lives. May we always treasure and care for the amazing body in which we dwell. We pray in the name of Jesus, Amen.

LECTIO DIVINA WITH SCRIPTURE

In the beginning was the Word, and the Word was with God, and the Word was God. He was in the beginning with God. All things came into being through him, and without him, not one thing came into being. What has come into being in him was life, and the life was the light of all people. The light shines in the darkness, and the darkness did not overcome it. (John 1:1-5, NRSV)

Contemplative Moments with Scripture

Divine Reading

LECTIO

Heart listens

Word shimmers

Spirit dances

Hope lifts into

MEDITATIO

Life learning

Lessons applying

Illuminations becoming

Heart filling into

ORATIO

Prayers lift

Hope rises

Petitions speak

Word becomes now

CONTEMPLATIVO

Silence shifts

Breath slows

Thoughts fall

Heart opens.

Lectio Divina with Scripture

In a very cerebral culture, words scroll across the screen to teach us. Perhaps we don't read as much anymore, but we absorb images and sound bites. Advertisements, political script, fashion images are a common diet these days. We who read perhaps do it for enjoyment, art, escape, and for information. In the contemplative approach, however, we read in a different way. Leaving behind these other ways, we take time to savor and reflect upon the words.

Preliterate people told stories. Scripture of the ancient ones lived in their hearts before they became words on parchment and later paper. Common people who didn't read relied on the spiritual leaders to read the holy words out loud. Words were carefully copied from one document to another. The monks were often the caretakers of the Christian scriptures in this way.

Over time, as more people learned to read, they began to read the scripture for themselves. The oral tradition, now written, helped them to learn about faith experiences in the past. Scriptures are read, discussed, dissected, researched, and interpreted. A common practice in most Christian churches will be for a preacher to speak on various scriptures each Sunday. Bible studies help teach the scripture and the meanings, interpretations.

But back in the 6th century, Benedict of Nursia started a meditative approach to scripture. Instead of reading and studying the passages, he began to instruct the monks to also pray with the scripture. This approach, known as *Lectio Divina*, was formalized into a four-step process in the 12th century by a Carthusian monk, Guigo II. In later years, the Catholic Church recommended it as a way to read scripture. Although there are variations on the approach, the main goal is to read scripture slowly, listening for God's word in a phrase or single word, rather than looking at the passage as a whole, in context.

You begin this practice by selecting a passage of scriptures. Psalms work well. Usually, you begin by reading the scripture through once or twice out loud. This is the first step: *Lectio* (reading). During the readings, you listen for what "shimmers" or jumps out at you on this particular day. You allow the Spirit to call your attention to something. It could be a word, a sentence, a phrase.

After you have focused on a particular part of the scripture, you move into *Meditatio* (meditating), during which you reflect on the word or words deeply. What is the message for your life today? What are you hearing? What drew you to that word?

Once you have a sense of the message for you, move on to the third step of *Oratio* (praying). During this time, pray over whatever you've discovered here, and how this message speaks to your life. Pray for that thought to take root in your every day.

Finally, you end your prayer by sitting in silence during the *Contemplativo* (contemplating) step. Let your thoughts go and just be present to God. The Latin words used to describe these steps don't quite vibe with our understanding of the words. The contemplative step is actually what most of us now refer to as meditation. If you have a regular meditation practice, you can begin your practice with this divine reading approach as preparation, which is probably how the monks originally conceived of the process.

A Letter from the Earth on Lectio Divina 1/6/19

Dear One,

My words resonate with your soul.

You humans compose all kinds of things with your thoughts, but in your sacred scripture, the words sing in ways not often found in other writing. So they can help guide you into my light.

I've been trying to teach you my way, which is to slow down, savor and appreciate.

Imagine a feast before you. You can gorge yourself with all sorts of delectable dishes and desserts and miss the unique tastes of the single servings. So it is with scripture. You might learn and be enlightened by a scripture passage but miss the gems of the holy words within.

So take time to listen like the monks of old and allow the scripture to shine into your heart and illumine your life. Then you will truly live the love and hope and joy for which you were born.

Love, Gaia

Nancy's Thoughts on Lectio Divina with Scripture

My own spiritual journey includes deepening meaning over time. I look for opportunities for new spiritual understanding. After years of reading scripture, there are many passages I have read and heard discussed hundreds of times. It's so important for me to have ways to keep the scripture fresh for me. *Lectio Divina* provides an awesome path for me to listen again for the first time with new ears, from my heart.

Listen to Gaia! Isn't she amazing in how She describes and encourages us in this process? As a writer, I find there are so many words on the pages. In these days, millions of books are being published. Many have great messages, tell incredible stories, and yet it can be too much. Even the Bible sometimes becomes just so many words and familiar stories.

Here, Gaia asks me to savor scripture in the way She's

asking me to savor all of life. She's very consistent in what she's been telling me! Slow down, appreciate, savor. And I find that doing this *Lectio Divina* approach with scripture opens the passage up to me in new ways. When I try this, I hear the voice of God in my life. When I've done it with a group, the same thing happens.

What follows is one of my personal prayer experiences with *Lectio Divina*, using the lectionary during Lent.

Lectio Divina with my Morning Meditation Lectio. It's morning time. I gather my journal, my Bible and pen, turn on the heater beside me and open the Holy Book

The Sinai Jesus, 4th century AD to the passage for this week of Lent, Psalm 63. I read the verses carefully, looking for words that shimmer, looking for a word from God for my soul this new day. As I come near the end of the Psalm, I find verses that speak to me. "I will instruct you and teach you the way you should go: I will counsel you with my eye upon you." I read the Psalm again and find myself drawn again to these two lines. Yes, that's what I need right now. During Lent this year, I began a small group to listen for direction on a mission project. This passage reminds me to trust God and we will be led. Those are the words that lift out and speak to my heart.

Meditatio. I pick up my pen and write. "*Be open to training. Watch. Take advantage of opportunities to learn. God's eye will be upon me. Place myself in God's presence. God warms me with love, connecting and watching over me.*" I remember the eyes of the Sinai Christ connecting with me during times of silent retreat, Taizé services, and now prayer time in my living room. And I feel comforted and know I am called to trust that God will open the way to me. My friends and I are participating in a Lent group, exploring possibilities of a mission project together. I realize I must continue to trust and listen and find the way.

Oratio. I pray, "*Teach me, God, and guide me. Counsel me. Lead me. I open myself to You. Help our group discern the path to goodness. Amen.*"

Contemplativo. I ring my singing bowl and sit into silence, imagining the eyes of God resting on me in love, absorbing the hope and joy of knowing the way will unfold.

Suggestions for *Lectio Divina* in Personal Practice

1. If you have a regular meditation or prayer practice, try using *Lectio Divina* for a week to begin your prayer or meditation time. This is very well suited for those who meditate, because it ends in a meditation. Write the four steps on a piece of paper with their descriptions to help guide you, if you are not familiar with the process.

2. After you practice *Lectio Divina*, take time to journal about the words that shimmered, how you applied them to your life, and what your prayers were concerning this. The journaling helps you remember the time in the future and may help deepen your experience.

3. If you attend a church that follows the lectionary, you can easily look these scriptures up on the internet and use them in your prayer time. You can take the bulletin home and continue to use the scriptures from the most recent week, or you can find the scripture for the following week and use them. Bringing the scripture into your personal practice will deepen the meaning of the worship time. Or if your church doesn't follow the lectionary, just use the scripture from the service in your reflection.

4. You can find particular scriptures for certain situations by doing searches online and use one that fits what's happening in your life. There are some suggestions for selecting verses in the appendix

.

An Experience of Lectio Divina for a Group

Introduction. Begin with a short introduction to *Lectio Divina* (5 minutes)

Body Prayer. Lead the group in 5 minutes of chanting the word "Shalom." Shalom is a Hebrew word meaning peace, harmony, and wholeness. Encourage them to let the word be a breath prayer for the body, mind and spirit. Set a slow pace. Instruct them to breathe in on the first syllable… "Shaaal"….taking in the breath throughout the body, visualizing the Spirit of God enlivening the body. On the outbreath, chant the second syllable, "ommmmm..," extending the word out as long as possible. You can continue chanting in unison, or have each person go at their own pace, creating a chorus of Shaloms.

Lectio Divina with Scripture. Choose a scripture verse for the group to read. You could choose a scripture on your theme, or perhaps from the lectionary for the week. Search online if you need ideas for a particular group.

Lectio. Explain that you will read the scripture through once slowly and ask the people to listen for the word or phrase that speaks to them. After the first reading, do a second reading.

After the second reading, give the group a chance to share the word or phrase that they heard. They can each speak their word or phrase into the circle.

Meditatio. Now ask the group to meditate and ruminate on what that word or phrase means to them today. What is the divine message coming through for their life? What guidance or illumination is provided to them?

After 2-3 minutes, give the group a chance to share the messages they hear for their lives.

Oratio. After this sharing time, instruct the group to spend some time in prayer, asking for God to help let this teaching take root in their lives. Explain that in 2-3 minutes, you will ring a bell to enter into the fourth step, or *Contemplativo*, during which they can sit in silence.

Contemplativo. Allow five minutes of silence and then ring the bell again.

Journaling. After this experience, provide the group with 10 minutes of journaling time. Provide some questions for them to consider, such as these:

1. In what ways did this time of prayer assist you in your connection with God?

2. What gifts or insights did you receive during this time?

3. Is *Lectio Divina* something that you want to continue to practice in your spiritual life? Why or why not?

Sharing. Provide a time for people to share about this experience at the end of the journaling time. (10 minutes).

LECTIO DIVINA WITH NATURE

Lectio Divina with the Birds

Monk Parakeets at White Rock Lake, Dallas, Texas

On the Sabbath,
On retreat, I open the Holy Book of Nature
And the birds preach to me.

These divine creatures
Are so far above my daily walk
And often beyond my consideration.

But this morning as I walk with God

They chirp and soar and I look up
To consider the birds, who spoke to Jesus; and now to me.

Soaring, gliding, flitting, chirping
Moving, singing, communicating
Interacting, perching, flying.

A realm of life above me
I watch, amazed
At their abilities to wing within the heavens.

I see you, God, there
In this community of wonder --
Diversity moving among the trees.

I hear their calls
I follow their voices
I don't understand, but I know you do.

And then I consider the birds
Becoming metaphor for prophets and saints
Who soar so high and preach good news.

I realize that I hope to learn
From those holy voices
And join their cacophony of hope.

The birds call me to listen and to learn
From those who have already learned how to fly.
And I hear the call to give voice to their truth.

My great work
Is to learn to fly with them
And to teach others how to soar.

As my morning worship ends
I watch the birds
And give thanks for their sacred Sabbath sermon from the sky.

Sunflowers at Tecumseh Land Trust Yellow Springs, Ohio

Contemplation is seeing God in everything and everything in God with completely extraordinary clearness and delicacy – Marie of the Incarnation

The natural world provides the contemplative a space for cultivating awareness of the Divine. When one walks into the Holy Book of Nature, there are miracles to discover in every step. Here, one glimpses the Creator's wisdom, intelligence, and creativity.

In our post-modern world, we often dwell in office environments, and even in our homes, we are surrounded with technology and equipment, gadgets and machines, papers and walls. Brian Swimme[13] suggests that much of the reason we have so much depression in our materialistic culture is that we focus too much on "dead things." We separate ourselves from a close connection with the earth. For this reason, perhaps, we allow our society to destroy much of the environment on which we depend. Regular walks in nature can begin to remedy this alienation and help lead to a path of personal and planetary healing.

---

[13]Brian Swimme. *The Hidden Heart of Cosmos: Humanity and the New Story*. New York City, New York: Orbis Books, 1996.

When one opens the door and takes a walk out into nature, the goal becomes once again mindfulness and awareness. Not to focus on a brisk walk, but to slow down and use the senses to see, hear, feel, smell and taste the infinite varieties of diversity in this amazing world.

Lectio Divina, a practice for reading scripture, can also be used to read the holy Word of God found in all of creation. Beginning with *Lectio* (reading), look at or "read" the landscape and listen for what "shimmers" or jumps out at you on this particular day. Allow the Spirit to call your attention to something. It could be the big picture, or a small decaying leaf; a flying bird or a stream of industrious ants. Then move into *Meditatio* (meditating) on that aspect of the Divine Word, considering the message for your life today. What are you hearing? Why did you happen to focus on that particular aspect of nature? After a time of meditation, move into *Oratio* (praying), for whatever you've discovered about a message for your life. Pray for that thought to take root in your every day. And finally, sit or walk with *Contemplativo* (contemplating), silencing your thoughts and just be present to God.

A walk in nature not only can heighten our awareness of God, but our physical interaction with the creation provides life-giving oxygen for us, and necessary carbon dioxide for the plants. This stimulates a harmony of mind, body and spirit.

When it's not possible to go on a walk outdoors, meditating on an indoor plant or even a photo of the natural world can provide contemplative joy.

Letter from the Earth on Lectio Divina with Nature 1/12/19

Winter: Rose bushes in my Mothers' Garden

Dear One,

Listen to the natural world with your heart.

There is so much going on outside your window on any given day. How often do you walk outside and get into your car without even noticing?

When I ask you to wake up, Nancy, I want you to wake up to the beauty into which you were born. I want you to give thanks and be attentive to the miracles of life.

Just look at your hand and be mesmerized. Ball it into a fist and then open your fingers. Let them flutter. Really look. Observe the usefulness. Imagine what lies under the skin. Quite amazing, isn't it?

Right now, it's winter for you, and so you hurry when you are outdoors. You think there is nothing to see, but that is so not true. Consider the trees. Stark beauty against changing skies, a testament to versatility that they can live through frigid temperatures. Can you let them teach you?

Consider those barren rose plants in your front garden. Prickly sticks, *now seemingly dead – and yet in a few months leaves will come and then my gorgeous pink and yellow fragrant Knockout roses, you know? Possibility just waiting its turn. Could they teach you patience?*

Ugly brown earth, frozen now in the winter cold. Yet you know, if you think about it, as soon as the warming trend starts, your bulbs will send up shoots into the air, and soon bright yellow daffodils, brilliant red tulips, delicate purple crocuses, and fragrant pink hyacinths will emerge. The earth holds promise, caretaking bulbs, and seeds of possibilities.

You see, Dear One, you must slow down, observe, watch, and listen for the love and messages of all creation. Open your heart and you will see.

I guarantee you will have a splendid time.

Love, Gaia.

Nancy's Thoughts on Listening to the Earth

Cypress Trees at Kelly's Lake, Ferncliff Cemetery and Arboretum, Springfield, Ohio

Listening to the Earth transforms my life. If there's anything in this book that I hope you will take seriously and incorporate more into your life, it's this process of paying attention to the natural world. Even as I write this, I know I don't do it enough.

When I received this letter from Gaia, I felt busted. Yes, winter brings gray days and stark views. Everything is coming up brown outside in Ohio where I live. She's right. I rush, and I don't spend time looking at the scenery. In fact, my inner critic tells me it's ugly and depressing. But, always, Gaia teaches me to open my perspective. She's quite amazing that way.

I do like the black branches of trees etching out onto the canvas of a white sky in winter. And after I received this letter, I started noticing the trees around me. I thought about their resilience and how they endure this season, hunkering down for the cold and ice. As I walked around my yard, I thought how they teach me to weather through the rough times of life.

After I read this letter, I looked at my hand with delight. So miraculous, this body in which I live and move and have my being. So far beyond comprehension, really.

And then our first major snow arrived. When they canceled church, I took my camera out for a walk. I photographed the rose bush in the snow. Truly amazing to observe thorned branches springing up from a fluffy white mound and to know in a few months, the energy of that plant and the sun would again produce green leaves, then beautiful, fragrant roses. In the nearby arboretum, I photographed tree after tree, displaying their beauty against a blue sky, draped in white. I breathed in the fresh, crisp air and felt enlivened by the gift of life and my connection with nature. Once again, I felt such deep gratitude to God for writing me letters, teaching how to live my life more vibrantly.

I believe that as a person slows down and begins a contemplative practice, they start to connect with the Earth in a deeper way. I know that to be true for me. I don't think it's accidental. I think it's because we are a part of the natural world. But we are also very cerebral beings, living in a material world, and we are distracted by much of modern culture. We forget to notice and pay attention. When we meditate, we let go of attachments to the things and thoughts and even feelings and dwell in the mystery of creation. When we walk the labyrinth, our bodies circle in symmetrical patterns, common to nature, connecting us to the rhythm of Earth. When we practice gratitude, we often are drawn to the miraculous unfolding all around us in plants and trees and people and landscapes and love. When we eat mindfully, we realize the gifts of the Earth, the plants, the creatures, and we marvel at how they sustain our lives.

As we notice Earth, we also in this day and age must acknowledge that our post-industrial society wreaks havoc on the intricate ecological systems which have developed and sustained life here for so long. The scientists tell us that our Earth evolved into such biodiversity over 4.7 billion years. I see the patience of a loving God who presides over such an amazing, evolutionary process. And I feel alarm that we humans have so much power to destroy that which developed over eons of time. As we awaken deep within, I believe we also hear the cry of the Earth to speak up, to take action, to join the millions of people asking for change to address the ecological issues we face.

For this reason, when I lead retreats and do public speaking, I always speak for the Earth. Right now, we must mobilize to address climate change. I encourage you to get involved as much as you can. Thomas Berry, a Catholic priest, wrote so prophetically when he told us that we are in the Ecozoic Age, during which we must change the way in which we relate to the Earth. He wrote, "We must walk together into the future as sacred community, or we will perish in the desert."

Suggestions for Personal Practice

1. Incorporate *Lectio Divina* with Nature into your contemplative practice, by including it at least once a week in your prayer time. When possible, go outside to do this. But also, you can do this indoors with a house plant, a photograph of nature, a flower bouquet, or just sitting by the window, looking outside. Follow the four steps. *Lectio*. "Read" nature by observing it very closely and consider what shimmers for you. *Meditatio*. Reflect on that shimmering aspect. How does it speak to you and your life? What's the message here for you? *Oratio*. Pray over this message, asking for it to take root in your life in some way. *Contemplativo*. Slip into silence with this new awareness and meditate for a few minutes.

2. Set an intention of noticing nature more in your life.

3. Do you have any house plants? If so, visit them each day and notice their changing lives. As you prune and water them, talk with them. Some research suggests that plants are aware of humans and respond to the vibrations of voice. They use your carbon dioxide and provide oxygen in return. Take good care of them and let them speak to you.

4. Take time each day for a short walk outside. Even it's only a minute or two, take time to look at the sky, the earth, a tree, a plant.

5. Make some Earth Prayer beads and use them as a rosary to pray daily for the Earth and your involvement with caring for the Earth. (See directions in the appendix).

6. If you like to journal, include your observations of nature. If you go for a nature walk, write down your experiences when you return. When possible, go outside to write.

7. If you like to take pictures, let the camera help you focus on

nature. Use the zoom and close-up scene mode to capture the intricacy of nature. In the spring, take pictures of the buds. If you like to garden, take pictures at different stages. Work on creating art with the natural world.

8. Cultivate the earth. Plant a flower garden or vegetable garden. Let this be part of your contemplative practice. Be mindful as you tend the garden. Rather than seeing your gardening as a chore, think of it as a time to become one with creation.

9. If you are an artist, let the Earth be a subject for you in your drawing, painting, writing, musical creations, photography, video productions. Find ways to let it speak to and through you as you create.

10. Look for ways to care for the Earth. Consider personal actions you can take in your everyday life.

11. Look for ways to speak up for the Earth in our collective lives. Join an environmental organization. Join Citizens' Climate Lobby (citizensclimatelobby.org). Be creative and vigilant, looking for the many platforms you personally have to speak for the Earth.

An Experience with the Trees

Branching Out, Buck Creek State Park, Ohio

Every fall, the women in my church head out to Buck Creek State Park for a weekend away. We rent several cabins close to the lake and spend most of the time socializing. Someone builds a campfire. We bring our favorite foods. Relationships deepen over hikes by the water, scavenger hunts around the cabins and games in the evening. We share stories, we sing and we absorb the beauty of the changing seasons. Usually, I lead a contemplative time on Saturday morning. Often, I've incorporated *Lectio Divina* with the Earth. We can walk right outside the cabin to open the Holy Book of Nature. Others less mobile sit inside gazing out through the window to the woods and lake.

A few years back, I introduced this exercise for the early risers, then hit the chime of my singing bowl to begin our time of *Lectio Divina*. Letting go of my leadership responsibility, I stepped out the door and slipped into the splendor of God's creation. Red, brown, yellow, and green leaves painted the ground's canvas with a bountiful tapestry of autumn. Above, golden light danced through translucent leaves forming a canopy over the cul-de-sac of cabins underneath. The whole world seemed to be shimmering and I looked for God's message to me on this day.

Yes, so beautiful this natural reality, and yet my heart felt heavy within me. As I awaken to the reality of our changing climate, sometimes I am just depressed. I try to speak, to organize with my husband, and to join others calling for action. Often it feels like we can't do enough, never enough. So, while I found myself immersed in splendor, a cloud of doom circled around me.

In the midst of my concern, I scrutinized the scene for hope. And suddenly, it jumped out. The trees! Branching out, rooting deep, hunkering down for winter now in a blaze of glory, growing wildly adapting to this little corner of earth. There they were, speaking, the voice of God to me that day. I stood with them, enjoying their strength, resourcefulness, beauty and drive.

When I gathered the group back inside a few minutes later, I rang the singing bowl again to enter a time of journaling and reflection. I picked up my pen and these words lifted out of my heart onto the paper:

The Wisdom of the Trees

I come asking for hope this day.
I come to listen to the nature of creation.
I come to open my senses into morning.
I come to learn.

Here, in this little bit of State Park heaven
I walk mesmerized by the beauty
Stretching up, out, and all around –
The sweet, answering wisdom of the trees.

I worry about the earth's destruction.
The trees simply grow.
They branch out and hunker down.
With variety, with resourcefulness and stride.

I worry how we will continue.

And then I watch the trees, cycling into autumn.
Their leaves blaze into glory, and let go,
Falling back down to earth.

I wonder what I can do –
And then I see the trees growing wildly, exploring possibilities,
Expanding to fill open space,
Each fulfilling their unique destiny.

I sense great chaos in our time,
And then I feel the strong trunk and rough bark.
I hold the strength of this towering giant,
Deeply rooted in earth.

I remember Hushpuppy listening[14]
And I open my ears and skin to the wind blowing through the trees
Feeling, hearing breeze, I watch
Trees swaying flexibly, in the flow.

I tend toward anxiety
But here I see trees simply being
Expressing their destiny in a great variety of greens, yellows, reds and browns;
Creating beauty in this landscape, microcosm of all.

I feel overwhelmed,
And then the trees tell me: Breathe in our oxygen offering.
I receive, and then breathe out; giving them carbon dioxide.
Yes, we are all interconnected -- we are one.

I ask for hope in our time
And the trees answer

---

[14] Hushpuppy was a character in the movie, "Beasts of the Southern Wild" (2012) documenting the Katrina hurricane. She was a 6-year-old girl who listened to nature in the film.

Branching mystery, growing toward life-giving light,
Rooting to God Spirit deep in earth, leading way.

I ring the singing bowl one more time, and we share out of our silence. Once again, Spirit speaks as we listen to the variety of ways that the Holy Book of nature teaches us about life. One feels love, another experiences goodness, one finds ways to greet the change and I rest into the moment, sharing my poem, trusting the Earth and its people to find a way through.

An Experience of a Contemplative Nature Walk for a Group

Serpent Mound in southern Ohio on the Spring Equinox welcomes walkers

Introduction. Begin with a short introduction to contemplative awareness in creation and using *Lectio Divina* to "read" the Holy Book of Nature. (5 minutes)

Body Prayer. Provide a guided meditation taking a journey inside the body and then outside into the marvels of the universe and back. (5 minutes) See pages 138-139 for script.

Lectio Divina in Nature. Send the group out on a walk, in nature, with instructions to try out *Lectio Divina* in the following way (20 minutes):

> 1. *Lectio – Reading with the heart. Listening for the aspect that shimmers or speaks especially to you. Observe the natural world and let God speak to you through some aspect of what you see, hear, feel, smell, and/or taste.*
>
> 2. *Meditatio – Reflect on that element that shimmers and turn it over in your mind. Meditate on its importance in your life.*

What is that message for you today?

3. *Oratio – Pray over your reflection; whatever God is speaking to you, what it's calling forth in you and your life.*

4. *Contemplativo – Sit or walk with God in silence with nature.*

Journaling. After people return from the nature walk, encourage journaling with these questions: (10 minutes)

1. In what ways did this time of prayer assist you in your connection with God?

2. What gifts or insights did you receive during this time?

3. Is *Lectio Divina* with nature something that you want to continue to practice in your spiritual life? Why or why not?

Sharing. Provide a time for people to share a gift of awareness from their walk.

Group Response: Thanks be to God for the gift of awareness.

Alternative to walking, or for any who would prefer to stay indoors: Hidden Things Photo Meditation

1. Choose a nature photo. Take some time to select the photo. Which one seems to be speaking to you this morning?

2. After you've chosen your photo, spend time just sitting with it and observing the miracle of God's creation while listening to "Hidden Things" (on *Sounds of the Eternal* by J. Phillip Newell) (10 minutes)

3. Journal about your experience with the photo.

Questions for reflection during journaling (10 minutes):

   a. What did you notice about nature while observing

this picture?

b. In what ways do you see God in this picture?

c. What amazes, surprises, confuses, astounds you about this aspect of nature?

Body Prayer: Nature Walk Prelude

A suggested script for a guided meditation of considering the miracles of creation, both inside the human body and within the whole of creation to lead into a time of walking in nature.

Script: Before we go for our walk, we are going to take a moment to be aware of our bodies and their place in this amazing universe in which we dwell. So we're going to go on a guided imagery journey inside your body, and then outside your body into this place where we'll walk soon, and then out into the heavens in which we dwell on our little planet. Get in a comfortable position and close your eyes. Take a few deep breaths and let them out slowly and relax. Place your hand on your heart. Can you feel it beating? Consider the work it does for you, even as you sit and relax. It takes the air you breathe from your lungs and helps circulate it through your bloodstream. Take a moment to consider the inner workings of your body. The circulatory system, circulating blood throughout your body with the faithful beating of your heart. The skeletal system, providing support for your body – your skull, and neck, your shoulders and ribs, your arms and hands, your hips and legs, your feet. Consider the digestive system, beginning with your mouth and teeth, the esophagus, the stomach, the small and large intestines. All making it possible for you to survive with its service every time you eat something. Consider your senses, how your nose and brain work together to enable you to smell fragrances, and the aroma of a delicious meal. Consider your eyes, how they work with your brain to allow you to see. Consider. Consider your hands and other body parts that touch and feel. Consider your ears, how they work with your brain to enable you to hear. Just take a few moments to breathe deeply, aware of the complex, miraculous systems within your body that give you life. (Pause) Now let's move out of this place into the outdoors. Notice the shape of the scenery, the ground, the trees, the horizon in this place. What do you see? Feel? Hear? Now imagine that you are able to fly. Start to float up above this place and look down. Soon, you are high enough to see the whole city or town in which you live. As you fly higher, the city becomes smaller and smaller and you start to see the larger region in which you live, the rivers and lakes, until suddenly, you start to also see the oceans. As you move up into the heavens, now you can see the planet as a whole, as you've seen pictures taken from space, now you see it with your own eyes. And you continue to move up into the heavens and you see the darkness and the lights of thousands of stars. You enter into the mystery of the universe. You see stars exploding in supernova events like the one that created our earth. You see stars burning up and meteors flying. You see our planets circling our star sun. You float in the mystery of it all. Now you start to float back down toward planet Earth. Once again, you see the small ball suspended in orbit around the sun, and as you get closer, you see the oceans and then the land, your country, your region, lakes and rivers, and now your city/town comes into focus and then you find yourself floating right back down into the area from which you came, landing on the earth, right outside your door.

You come back inside and once again you sit, in your body, in this room. But now, you think for a moment of both the inner workings of your miraculous body and your place in this amazing universe. Try to keep this in your mind's eye as you take a walk outside in a few minutes. Now, when you're ready, open your eyes.

MINDFUL MEALS

Mindful Meal

On silent retreat
Meals offer meaning,
Mindful practice,
New dimensions of digestion.

Savor completely.
Chew slowly.
Focus awareness
On inner transformations.

Consider planting, nurturing,
harvesting, slaughtering,
packaging, transporting,
selling/buying, preparing.

How many people, plants, animals
To thank?
How many hands
Contributed to the bounty of this plate?

Lay down the fork after each bite.
Then chew, reflect,
Remember, give thanks
And start over again.

Marvel at the gifts.
Enjoy the colors.
Recognize exquisite composition.
Hold gratitude for edible blessings.

Find time to pray
For those present and afar.

Find time for
Simple enjoyment.

How can it be
A meal yields such profound practice?
How can it be
Mindfulness brings such peace?

The Gift of Contemplative Meals

Contemplation is looking at life as it is in in the very here and now.

– Thich Nhat Hanh

On retreat, an opportunity for contemplative silence comes at mealtime. Such an ordinary experience of breaking bread together becomes infused with spacious meaning and holy presence when words are left behind.

Choosing to eat mindfully involves eating slowly and savoring the food. Noticing the colors, the tastes and textures can be quite astounding. Suddenly, the table becomes a living sanctuary, full of the glory of creation.

A contemplative meal provides a special time for gratitude. There is time to consider the long chain of growth and activity leading to the presence of food on the table. There is time to consider and give thanks for the people who planted and harvested, packaged and transported, prepared and presented the food. There is time to consider and give thanks for the varieties of plants and animals that grew into fullness and now offer a gift of life at your table.

A contemplative meal provides a laboratory to practice mindfulness and dwelling in the present. Putting down the utensil between each bite can help foster slowing down. Really paying attention to each morsel provides more time for the digestive process. Your body benefits and your soul enjoys the delight.

Some retreatants may feel the silent meal creates a barrier to communication with companions at the table. But observing silence also provides a bridge to deeper connection among people. Silent prayers may be offered for others in the room. A sense of parallel journeys may become evident. New awareness of the other may arise. Letting go of words provides new freedom in community.

For those new to silence at meal time, preparation may involve a brief introduction prior to the meal. Simple instructions on the table can encourage prayer and mindfulness with each bite.

A Letter from the Earth on Eating Mindfully 1/8/18

Dear One,

Do you realize that the food you eat is a gift from me to you? Every morsel, every bite is such a miracle supporting your existence.

Slow down and appreciate the miracle, please. You humans are forgetting to take time for the important things these days. You rush, rush, rush, for what? Stop.

For eons, my people have honored food with many rituals, giving thanks, sitting together, reclining even, around the table, savoring the offerings of Earth. Now, you package my offerings with preservatives and grab bites on the go and you forget to observe the sacred experience of a meal.

Slow down. Stop, if you will, every time you eat, Dear One. Eat slowly. Savor each bite. Acknowledge flavors, textures and the joy.

Give thanks not only for the meal, but for each person who brings it to your table. The farmer, the rancher, those who toil in the sun, the packagers, the transporters, the store employees, the shopper. Give thanks for each plant, each animal offering its life for you.

Consider the miracle of the digestion process that turns these offerings of Earth into fuel for your life. Quite amazing, isn't it, Dear One?

So slow down. Eat mindfully. Be thankful. Be aware of the miracles overflowing from the earth to your table becoming your body now. Your life will take on a whole new quality. Your spirit will soar. You will realize, once again, how very much I love you.

Your friend, Gaia.

Nancy's thoughts on Eating Mindfully

Wow. Gaia's getting a little perturbed with me, I think, in this letter! It makes me laugh, and also cry, as I feel the truth of her words. I feel goosebumps forming, as I consider her deep wisdom. Yes, I hear her. I know what she is saying is so true, and yet it's also a lesson I'm very slow to learn.

Throughout my life, a family meal offered an anchor for each day. As a child, we waited for my father to come home, and we always dined together, said a prayer and then enjoyed my mother's cooking as we talked about the experiences of our lives. Spaghetti, roast beef, mashed potatoes, grilled cheese sandwiches with tomato soup, tater tots and my mom's specialty of "porcupine balls" – meatballs infused with rice (the spines), cooked in a tomato sauce within her pressure cooker. Always a balanced meal, always thoughtfully prepared by my mom. How well I remember the food my mother prepared for us. As parents, my husband and I followed this tradition as much as possible. We would gather at 6 p.m. for dinner. Even when my husband worked the evening shift, he would take his dinner time early to sit with us. Later, my husband taught my sons to cook during the summers, when he was home in the mornings with them. We enjoyed each other's concoctions and experiments. They say that this simple practice helps set children on a good course in their lives. Families eating together are less likely to have children that end up going astray with drugs and such.

Over time in my now empty nest life, food is not so important to me. At my house, the evening meal slipped into decline and almost nonexistence, as my aging body doesn't need much sustenance in the latter part of day. I prepare breakfast at home, but eat it at my desk at work, while doing other things. I fill my lunch hour with exercise, a music group and Toastmasters, and then eat my food again at my desk while working in the afternoon.

Last year, my husband retired, and now he's starting to carve a time for us together in early evening with creative meals. I'm gaining weight. I tell him I'll eat this for my lunch the following day. But, now, as I listen to Gaia's chiding, I realize that I need to sit and savor with him. And not be in a hurry for what? I laugh at myself. No, I don't need to hurry at night.

The first time I considered eating mindfully came as I read Thich Nhat Hanh, the Vietnamese Buddhist who has written so many books on practicing mindfulness. I remember once taking his book to the table with me, reading his directions on mindfulness and then slowly eating and savoring each bite. It's amazing how different food can taste when you slow down. You can really appreciate the varieties of fruits and vegetables, the textures.

But the time I really learned to eat mindfully happened on a silent retreat. When I attended the Shalem Institute for Spiritual Formation program on leading contemplative small groups and retreats, we gathered for residencies. Always, there would be a silent retreat as part of this training, when for a day and a half or two, we entered into the silence. A silent retreat is a powerful experience, which I highly recommend, by the way. But also, during the silent retreat, we would still gather together at meal times, without speaking.

The first time, I remember placards on the tables. On one side, it told us to give thanks for the people who prepared the food. On the other, it included sentence phrases about mindfully eating. When you let go of words, you focus on so much more.

Suddenly, I began to think about the many people who bring food to my table. I imagined the wheat growing in the field, the beans on the plant, the fruit on the trees. I wondered about the animals who gave up their lives for my meal. I ate in awe of the food production process.

And I ate slowly, giving thanks, and in prayer for those without enough food. I prayed for the people at the table with me. It's really such an awe-inspiring experience. I think this is what Gaia is talking about. And I know I don't need to go on a silent retreat to do this.

After I received this letter from the Earth, I began experimenting. Always in a quest to lose weight, I decided to eat one Hershey kiss, instead of 4, and really savor it. I love sugar and chocolate, but I've found that the rush and enjoyment is possible with small quantities. I focus on the quality of the experience. Letting the kiss melt on my tongue, I enjoyed the soft texture of the chocolate, filling my taste buds with joy as the candy lingered in my mouth. Yes, I could get as much fulfillment from one, and perhaps more than eating a handful.

And a few weeks ago, I discovered a weight loss app called "Noom." Once again on a journey to shed unnecessary pounds, I've been finding it helpful as I log my weight each day and the calories in each meal. In addition to tracking my weight, calories and steps, the app provides many suggestions for how to think myself to better health. Imagine my surprise when "mindfulness" came up in the daily educational topics. I found myself pledging to eat mindfully by putting down my fork or spoon between bites. And when I remember to do this, I find myself enjoying my food so much more. And I'm actually losing weight!

In creating space in our lives, we slow down and realize the miracles of the moment, as Gaia said. She tells us to focus on the digestion process. If you really think about this, it's mind-blowing. Beginning with the taste of food, our nose and taste buds on our tongue allow us to truly experience the food we eat. Continuing with the saliva which starts to break down the food. Then our throat and swallowing process, carrying the morsels down the esophagus, specially designed to move the food along with tiny hairs as it continues its journey to our stomach, where more chemical processes turn it into energy to be carried through our blood stream, then pushing the waste into our small intestines, where the food continues to move into the large intestines, all the cells working together to move the waste along, until our body calls us to eliminate what is not needed. And the process begins again. The liquid gathers in our bladder for elimination. Don't we take this all for granted? But if you really start to think about your body and the work it does and then try to imagine how it came to be and how life is possible at all, you will find gratitude starting to swell up in that incredible beating heart of yours, and you will be blessed, as you already are.

My husband and I are enjoying evening meals together much more frequently, and he's experimenting with some low calorie recipes so I can eat happily and mindfully in the evening. I take delicious offerings to work, and even though I'm still eating at my desk so I can exercise and do other things during my lunch hour, I have found that putting down my spoon between sips, or my fork between bites, helps me slip into a contemplative moment for my spirit as my body finds nourishment as well.

Suggestions for Mindful Eating Personal Practice.

1. Make a placard for your table.[15] On one side, write: In this food, may I see clearly and gratefully the presence of the entire universe supporting my existence. All living beings are struggling for life. May each one have enough food to eat today. I vow to live for the benefit of all living beings. On the other side, write: THE FOUR GREAT ACTIONS. With the first taste, I promise to practice loving kindness. With the second, I promise to relieve the suffering of others. With the third, I promise to see others' joy as my own. With the fourth, I promise to learn the way of peace and presence.

2. Next time you eat a snack, eat it mindfully. Savor each bite. Really chew your food, noticing the texture and the taste.

3. If you tend to overeat, next time you approach something where you might eat 15-20 of, say, crackers or chips, select 4-5 and eat them slowly, enjoying the crunch and the taste and experience. Experiment and note if that fewer number is more satisfying than a large quantity.

4. If you are eating a meal alone, choose to give yourself time to really savor your food. Perhaps decide in advance to spend 30 minutes eating. Take single bites and savor the food as it goes down. Imagine what happened to get that food to your table. Consider your loved ones not dining with you and pray for them. Let each bite be a time for thanksgiving and prayer. Pray for those without enough food. Be present in the

---

[15] These cards were designed by Ann Dean who directs contemplative leadership programs for the Shalem Society for Spiritual Formation in Washington, D.C.

experience. Consider your digestive process. Approach your meal as an experience of participating in a miracle. When you slow down and take time, you encounter the sacred.

5. Focus more on eating whole foods, less processed food. When you prepare a meal, focus on quality, not quantity, and take time to really savor the meals.

6. If you dine regularly with your family or others, you might try a silent meal once a week, using the placard you designed. Or perhaps even just five minutes of silence, and then talk about what you noticed.

An Experience of a Contemplative Meal for a Group

Retreatants eat mindfully on Shalem silent retreat

Introduction. Begin with a short introduction to contemplative silence during a meal, and the practice of mindful eating. (2-3 minutes).

Body Prayer. Provide a guided meditation focusing on the body's digestion process. See page 154 for a suggested script (5 minutes).

Contemplative Eating. Provide a simple meal with a diversity of fresh fruits and vegetables, attractively presented. Place table tents with the instructions as suggested in #1 above in Suggestions for Personal Practice.

Journaling. Encourage journaling briefly after the meal on the following questions:

1) In what ways did the silent meal contribute to your awareness of God?

2) Were there any difficulties for you in this practice? What was that about?

3) Do you want to incorporate mindful eating and/or

maintaining silence during meals into your spiritual practice? Why or why not?

Sharing. Provide a time for people to share their experiences with the mindful meal.

Body Prayer: Guided Meditation on the Digestion Process

A suggested script for a guided meditation of the digestion process to heighten relaxation and awareness of the body, leading into a time of a silent meal and mindful eating. Place a plate of appetizers or fruit/crackers/cheese/nuts on the table in the center and invite each person to take something to eat for this meditation.

Before we eat our meal, let's take a moment to consider our digestive process. When we eat mindfully, we take time to really chew our food, savor it and also consider the amazing body system of ours that takes the food in, breaks it down and provides fuel for our living, discarding the waste products. Get in a comfortable position and relax. Hold the piece of food you've chosen in your hand. Close your eyes and take a few deep breaths in... and out... In... and out... In... and out... *(Take the breaths yourself to demonstrate and help pace yourself.)* In... and out... Consider for a moment the food you chose and what nutrition it will provide for your body. Now, take a bite of the food and chew it in your mouth. Consider your teeth that help break it into small pieces. Feel the saliva joining the food to ease its coming process through the body. What do you taste? Consider your tongue and your nose which enlist your brain to help you enjoy the taste of this food. When you're ready, swallow the food and feel your jaw and throat helping the food along into your esophagus. This tube contracts and expands to pass the food along. Consider its journey down this long tube. Right before the stomach, there is a valve or a high-pressure zone to keep the food from passing back up into the esophagus. As it passes into the stomach, it comes into this sac-like organ with strong muscular walls. The stomach holds the food and also begins to mix and grind the food. Now, it is secreting acid and powerful enzymes that continue the process of breaking down the food. When it leaves the stomach, food is the consistency of a liquid or paste. From there, imagine your food moving on into the small intestine. Here, there are three segments, the duodenum, jejunum, and ileum. All together, it's longer than 20 feet long.

Imagine the small intestine continuing the process of breaking down food by using enzymes released by the pancreas and bile from the liver. Bile is a compound that aids in the digestion of fat and eliminates waste products from the blood. Peristalsis or contractions are also helping here, moving food through and mixing it up with digestive secretions. The duodenum is largely responsible for continuing the process of breaking down food, with the jejunum and ileum being mainly responsible for the absorption of nutrients into the bloodstream. Consider your food making this journey through these 20 feet of small intestines, now releasing the nutrients into your bloodstream. Take time to notice the three organs that play a pivotal role in helping the stomach and small intestine digest food. The pancreas secretes enzymes into the small intestine. These enzymes break down protein, fat, and carbohydrates from the food we eat. The liver makes and secretes bile to cleanse and purify the blood coming from the small intestine containing the nutrients just absorbed. The gallbladder is a pear-shaped reservoir that sits just under the liver and stores bile. Bile is made in the liver. Then, if it needs to be stored, it travels to the gallbladder through a channel called the cystic duct. During a meal, the gallbladder contracts, sending bile to the small intestine. Once the nutrients have been absorbed and the leftover liquid has passed through the small intestine, what is left of the food you ate is handed over to the large intestine, or colon.

Now the 5-6 foot-long muscular tube of the colon connects the cecum to the rectum. Stool, or waste left over from the digestive process, is passed through the colon by means of peristalsis (contractions), first in a liquid state and ultimately in solid form as the water is removed from the stool. Your stool will be stored in the sigmoid colon until a "mass movement" empties it into the rectum once or twice a day. It normally takes about 36 hours for stool to get through the colon. The stool itself is mostly food debris and bacteria. These bacteria perform several useful functions, such as synthesizing various vitamins, processing waste products and food particles, and protecting against harmful bacteria. When the descending colon becomes full of stool, or feces, it empties its contents into the rectum to begin the process of elimination. And there you have it. This little bit of food you just ate will be processed by your body and then the waste will be moving out in about a day and a half. Let's pray. Thank you, God, for this amazing digestive system in our bodies. Help us to be ever aware and thankful for this amazing process. As we move into our time of mindful eating now, may you bless our time together. May we be aware of all who have brought our food to the table. May we be aware of this amazing process of digestion. May we be aware of those who share this time with us. Bless our food and our lives to your service. Amen.

COMMUNITY RITUALS

The Contemplative Gift of Group Rituals

"Nothing is more conducive to a communion with the living God than a meditative common prayer, as its high point, singing that never ends but continues in the silence of one's heart when one is alone again."

– Brother Roger, Taize

The contemplative community of Taize in northern France has been praying for peace and offering a space for silent prayer and worship for over 70 years. In the summer, thousands of young people flock to the small town from all over the world. Three times a day, the brothers and their guests gather to pray. Worship revolves around simple prayers, scripture readings and prayer song chants, accompanied by cello, acoustic guitar and recorder. The brothers of Taize sometimes travel to other countries, offering workshops to teach the music and pray for peace. Over time, the Taize chants have become popular in the United States.

On Fridays at Taize, a tradition of "Prayer Around the Cross" offers a special time of prayer, remembering Jesus' suffering. A large cross becomes the focal point for the service in which people lay burdens down at the cross.

A Taize service provides a contemplative alternative to traditional worship. Often conducted with candlelight, some churches offer this as an additional service during the week. Resources on the Taize[16] website teach how to organize the service and even provide the music for the songs.

---

[16]The website for the Taize Community can be found at Taize.fr, available in many languages, including English.

Taize Song[17]

Candles at Community Taize Service

"In the Lord I'll be ever thankful."

Gratitude swells beyond words.

"In the Lord I will rejoice."

Flickering candles radiate onto beloved community.

"Look to God, do not be afraid."

Sinai Jesus meets my gaze with compassion.

"Lift up your voices, the Lord is near."

I join the choir as I pull my bow across violin strings.

"Lift up your voices, the Lord is here."

Yes.

[17] The inspiration for this poem came from the Taize Song, "In the Lord, I'll Be Ever Thankful". copyright © Ateliers et Presses de Taizé, 71250 Taizé, France.

A Letter from the Earth concerning Community Ritual 1/4/19

Dear One,

Since the beginning of human existence, people have come together in ritual, often focused on Me, really. The seasons mesmerized early people. They watched the sun move and built structures to align. They knew the stars. They danced to welcome spring, they lit fires in the winter, giving thanks, and sending up smoke for petition. Ritual provides a way to come together, to participate in my mystery, to become a part of the cosmos, connecting with the energy of all life.

In these late days, you struggle to find meaningful rituals. Your young often leave the church behind in your country. The older people find comfort in the familiar worship structures in your churches, synagogues, and mosques.

I encourage you to practice both the new and the old. Be bold in creating new rituals that bring people together in new ways. Continue the old structures that bring hope to the elders. What's important is that your rituals connect you with each other and with Me, providing you sustenance for your journey.

Life can be very hard, Dear One. Community is good. Spiritual communities help you all light the darkness, hold a candle of hope, extend hospitality and move forward into joy.

Ritual is powerful, liberating, helpful, and necessary for life. Experiment, practice, be creative in these changing times. I will help you.

Love, Gaia

Nancy's Thoughts on Contemplative Ritual

When I received this letter from Gaia God, I appreciated the broad perspective of looking back in time at the ways people have used rituals. I love her suggestion to continue the old rituals, but also to build new rituals. I think this is so important in each time.

Things have changed very rapidly in my lifetime. Technology developed quickly. When I attended high school, computers were a very new thing. Now, they have become a part of almost everything we do. Yet our religious organizations sometimes are very slow to change, which can be comforting for us, even as they become increasingly irrelevant to a society that slipped into a new way of life in the past few decades.

When contemplative practice became important to me, I sometimes became frustrated with the ritual of the worship service in the churches I attend. Often, Christian worship leaves very little time for silence and dwelling in the mystery of God. I think it's a characteristic of the Western church to be extremely cerebral and less focused on the body and Spirit in worship. Sometimes this leaves very little room for the Spirit to speak and for the person to respond.

I've attended worship in many different places. Growing up as a preacher's kid in the Evangelical United Brethren Church, which became United Methodist, I regularly attended a traditional worship service with hymns, sermon, prayer and creeds. As I became an adult, I explored a variety of denominations. I attended a Unitarian church for a while, joined a Lutheran student community, then a Presbyterian church. I enjoyed attending a contemporary Mass at a Catholic student center for a while and then became a Mennonite, because of pacifist beliefs. Later, my family joined a Lutheran church and now an American Baptist Church. In a Global Education and Peace Network that I have facilitated for many years, we spent one year visiting places of worship of various traditions. So I have also bowed and prayed in a mosque, listened in a Sikh temple, meditated in a Buddhist meditation room, experienced a Hindu temple, attended a Baha'i meeting and worshiped in a synagogue.

As a contemplative, first I encourage you to find the moments of silence and contemplative joy in whatever rituals you already practice. In traditional Christian worship, there are usually musical interludes of a prelude, an offertory, and a postlude when you can enjoy the silence and mystery. Certainly, in a Buddhist, Hindu or Quaker worship space, you'll find long periods of silence. The liturgy offers mantras into silence. When the same words are repeated in every service, they can help guide you into a contemplative cadence.

I learned the Taize worship style in Iowa during my 20s, and then in my 50s, a local pastor brought Taize worship into our church in Springfield, Ohio. Just recently, we've begun a collaboration with six downtown churches, taking turns offering Taize worship monthly. There, we gather across denominational lines, with the silence and meditative chants bringing us together as one in a beautiful way. I enjoy playing my violin at these services.

Another ritual many find helpful is a contemplative prayer group, where you gather to meditate together. Many find an energy to meditating in a group.

The labyrinth offers a time of contemplative community ritual, as well. It can be used to commemorate birthdays, holy days, transitions, and just getting together to pray. Although the labyrinth walk is a quiet, personal journey, many find it meaningful to share that walk with others. The path of the labyrinth replicates many things we experience on the path of life. When we walk the labyrinth with others, it becomes symbolic of the way we each travel separately, and yet we're also traveling together. The labyrinth holds us all.

I believe that we do need new rituals in our time to help us experience the fullness of God. As a contemplative, I find those rituals that hold space for silence and interaction with God to be most liberating. Creativity and experimentation are needed to create helpful rituals moving us forward into life.

Suggestions for Your Personal Practice

1. If you already attend worship services, make a point to slip into silence when there are musical interludes, a prelude, offertory, postlude... all opportunities for contemplative time.

2. Attend a variety of worship services. Attend a Quaker meeting or a Buddhist meditation room.

3. Encourage your religious organization to incorporate more silence into worship.

4. Check out the Taize website at www.taize.fr/en. Learn some of the songs. Attend a Taize worship or organize one in your community. Visit Taize in France.

5. Join or start a meditation group where you gather to sit into silence once a week.

6. Attend or host a community time at the labyrinth.

Suggestions for Group Practice

Plan a contemplative Taize worship service. Enlist the help of musicians to play the music of Taize, which you can find on their website. You could also add a time of communion if you wish.

Take care to create an environment for contemplation. Arrange candles. Include holy icons if possible. Spend some time educating the congregation on contemplative worship. In many services, people are uncomfortable with times of silence. Explain that the silence can be used to meditate, to rest with God, to listen, and to pray silently.

See below example of a Taize order of worship. Notice the service flows between the chanting music, repeated 4-8 times and even more, scripture, prayer and silence. No sermons are offered. The message comes in the music, the words of scripture, and in the silence.

Opening Song	*In the Lord I'll Be Ever Thankful*
Silence	
Responsive Psalm	Psalm 19:7-14 NRSV
Sung Response	*Kyrie Eleison*
Silence	
Epistle Reading	James 5:13-20
Silence	
Gospel Reading	Mark 9:38-50 NRSV
Silence	
Song	*Bless the Lord, My Soul*
Prayers of Intercession	
The Lord's Prayer	
Song	*Stay with me*
Closing Song	*Let all who are thirsty come*

If possible, guide a time of reflection after the worship service. Give people a time to reflect on how the worship assisted their connection with God, what was helpful and what might be a struggle for them.

CONTEMPLATIVE LIVING

Contemplative Life

Meditate
> *and silence will open into dawn.*

Walk
> *and sacred path will guide into day.*

Connect
> *and sacred conversation will nurture you into hope.*

Give thanks
> *and joy will cascade into heart.*

Read Spirit
> *and message will light into way.*

Live mindfully
> *and transformations will unfold into good.*

Ritually gather
> *and community will carry you into God.*

Act from the Center
> *and hope will build into new possibilities.*

Dwell in sacred moment
> *and love will surround into sustaining life.*

About Contemplative Living

"To see a world in a grain of sand, and a heaven in a wildflower, hold infinity in the palm of your hand and eternity in an hour."

– William Blake

The spiritual life may jumpstart in a mountaintop experience, but it's fueled by daily practice, observation, and ritual that bring us into the heart of God as we live our lives. Those monks and cloistered nuns sequestered away in monasteries teach us much about how to cultivate a life with God, but for most of us, we need to apply the teachings in the stuff of every day where we dwell minute by minute. Here, God comes most fully alive in our awareness when we welcome God in.

Long ago, Jesus told us that the Kingdom of God is at hand. His stories and ministries teach us to love each person, welcoming them as the Christ. Within the contemplative journey, the Holy One also invites us to honor sacred time in each moment. With each step, we discover we tread on holy ground.

In our society, we learn delayed gratification. We work hard for a future reward. Some Christians approach their faith in the same manner. But contemplative practice teaches us, as William Blake wrote, to "see a world in a grain of sand, and a heaven in a wildflower, hold infinity in the palm of your hand and eternity in an hour."

Waking up means answering the call to be here now. When we are awake, we dare enter into the mystery of life as it unfolds. We look not only to future glories but find the glory in this day. We see miracles in our bodies, in other people, in the created world, in so many places.

In Richard Rohr's book, *The Universal Christ* (2019, page 119), he writes, "I doubt if you can see the image of God (*Imago Dei*) in your fellow humans if you cannot see it in rudimentary form in stones, in plants and flowers, in strange little animals, in bread and wine… It really ends up being all or nothing, here and then everywhere." To live contemplatively, one begins to realize each moment of our life is a time to encounter God.

Being contemplative also helps one deal with difficult experiences. Ruth King, in her book, *Mindful of Race: Transforming Racism from the Inside Out* (2018), explains a process called RAIN that she uses to deal with experiences of racism. First, one Recognizes what is going on. In experiences of systemic and individual racism, she recommends stepping back to analyze and consider what has happened and how it impacts you; how it makes you feel in your body. Then you move into a phase of Allowing whatever happened just to be. You just sit with it, observing both the reality of the situation and the horror of it, the anger it brings. After that, you move into the Investigation phase when you consider how you are relating to what is happening. Finally, you move into Nurturing yourself. She suggests that by using this process over time, experiences of racial distress can be clearly seen, interrupted, and attended to within the person, while providing clarity for action. Here, contemplative practice also helps care for self in the midst of oppression.

As we develop our contemplative life, we learn this importance of extending holy awareness beyond specific times set aside for spiritual practices. Yes, when we learn to cultivate contemplative awareness throughout the day, all moments become sacred time. Then we begin to realize that completing mundane chores becomes an opportunity for silence and prayer. We experience conversation drawing us into relationship with Christ in the other. We find that physical and mental labor provide space for welcoming Spirit. And then, we truly awaken into the heart of God in the center of our lives.

A Letter from the Earth about Living in the Moment

Dear One,

Your life unfolds in moments. Yes, the calendar pages seem to unfurl at a rapid rate, but really, you just live, moment by moment.

It's the moment where I challenge you to stay. Be fully present here, now.

Be aware of your surroundings. Be aware of the people. Take time to observe, listen, touch, use all of your senses. Feel.

Try not to be distracted with electronic devices all day long. When you attend a gathering, be present. When you're at work, show up with your full self. When you spend time with a person, be completely present, with them. Even when you are doing chores, you can be aware of the sacred.

Perhaps you're folding clothes? Take time to marvel at the garments in gratitude. Perhaps you're chopping carrots? Find joy in the color, texture, nutrition, miracle. Perhaps you're cleaning? Take time for prayerful reflection.

You can practice contemplative silence in so many moments of your day. Let the joy permeate your life. Let sadness speak. Let hope grow.

Show up. Be present. Listen and you will know.

Love, Gaia

Nancy's Thoughts about Contemplative Living

Yes! Once again, I receive a Letter from the Earth and once again, she speaks to my heart and leads me into right living. Doesn't she get it right? She tells us to stay in the moment. This, I believe, is the key to life. But our lives are filled with distractions these days, and it's so easy to go through the day distracted, reading social media, listening to the news, fingering our phones, playing games on our tablets, and missing the miracle of life.

As I write this chapter, I'm in the season of Lent. Christians often try to give up something for Lent to help focus on the suffering of Jesus. Some also suggest that doing additional spiritual practices during Lent helps retain focus on Jesus. I started a Mission Group for Lent and decided that was my Lent practice. But then yesterday, I thought about something else.

Since I was a child, I've played Scrabble. With my parents and brothers, later with friends and my husband. Even as my father lay dying, my mother and I kept a game going as we accompanied him to the end, taking turns talking with him and finding places to play the letters. When I installed Word with Friends, a Scrabble-like internet game, on my iPad a few years ago, I was ecstatic. Now I play all the time. The game offers many incentives to keep me hooked. I earn mystery boxes for milestones, colored tiles, free swaps, and word radar. I play with Facebook friends and email contacts. As Lent began, I'm competing with my nephew who lives in New York, my childhood friend who lives in Columbus, my grade school friend who lives in Texas, my retired pastor, my best childhood friend's mother, and the list goes on. They drew me in, and I'm addicted. Yesterday, a few days into Lent, I decided to give this game up until Easter. I explained it to the people with whom I'm playing and resigned each game, one by one.

Suddenly, I do feel more peaceful and less distracted. I find more time for the important things. I allow letting go of that to bring me into the presence of God, which I think this "giving up something" in Lent is all about.

For many years, I've enjoyed spiritual retreats, groups and church. I seek out spiritual learning in books. But, I also get frustrated when I enter into loving realms in these experiences and books, and then fall into disarray in my daily life. So, I look for little practices to keep me contemplative while walking through the day.

At work, I try smiling when I'm talking on the phone. I pray for God to send the people to me who need a listening ear. I seek to really hear the people who call me and visit. You know, we humans can be very difficult at times. The people who call and visit me while I'm at work are usually upset. Tenants rave about unresponsive landlords who won't fix things. No heat, plumbing issues, a leaking roof, cause havoc in their lives. Landlords also rage. The tenant doesn't pay their rent on time or at all. The tenant destroys their property. The tenant makes too much noise. I've heard it all. But, when I can really listen to the person and care about them as the Christ, it helps. I provide resources, not always solving their problems, but point them in directions for them to do what they can. Allowing contemplative space in the moment helps me listen better, care more, and in the long run, I believe, helps me serve them better as well.

Since I've become a contemplative, I find myself so much more aware of nature. I appreciate the clouds in the sky. I marvel at the varieties of weather. I absorb the sunshine, but also consider the rain and snow. The letters I've received from the Earth instruct me to go outside more and observe, and I do. Going for short breaks, walking outside can build contemplative space.

And meditation starts my day off well, but I find I can also take time to focus on my breath throughout the day. When I deal with a particularly difficult person, I get stressed. My body feels it. My heart beats more quickly, I feel agitated inside. If I take a few minutes to breathe deeply, I can center back into a good place, letting go of the stress and not carrying it with me the rest of the day.

It's an ongoing challenge to live contemplatively. The busier we are, the harder it gets and the more important it becomes to take breaks. How does one transform perspective from the tyranny of now to the possibilities of the sacred in the now?

This year, one of my goals is to slow down. Perhaps because I'm getting older and my body requires this of me, I choose this. But we must each learn to say no to the unimportant and to say yes to that which helps cultivate the sacred within. In this section, we consider ways to extend our contemplative practice into every moment.

Suggestions for Personal Practice

1. Unplug yourself. Give yourself a break each day from some of the electronic devices that control you. Turn off your phone. Put the tablet away. Turn off the TV.

2. Go outdoors. Take a break at least twice a day for some time outdoors. Observe nature. Try walking very slowly and meditatively with deep breaths.

3. Take a five-minute breath meditation break. Stop wherever you are and set a timer for five minutes. Focus on your breath. You might breathe in slowly, counting to 5 and then out, with the same count. Or if you prefer, use a mantra. You might just focus on God's presence. As you breathe in silently, think "You." As you breathe out, acknowledge "are with me." This helps extend the value of meditation throughout your day.

4. Journal about your discoveries of living in the moment and practicing the presence of God. Every day, take time to acknowledge and celebrate the special contemplative moments you shared when you experienced God in a person, in nature, in an experience or in breath.

5. Be present in relationship. Take time to really be with another person. Stop doing other things, and just listen. Connect with them through your body language and your heart. Consider the ways that other person is Jesus to you.

6. Practice the presence of God in simple chores. A monk, Brother Lawrence, worked in the monastery kitchen. He wrote a book he named *The Practice of the Presence of God*[18] about how his work provided countless opportunities to be with God in his food preparation, serving and cleaning up. Perhaps that chore

[18] Brother Lawrence of the Resurrection, 1611-1691. *The Practice of the Presence of God.* Available free online from The Christian Classics Ethereal Library. https://www.ccel.org/ccel/lawrence/practice.txt.

you hate could be an entry point to contemplative joy? Complete each task mindfully. Give thanks. Pray. Slip into the zone of silence. Be aware of God with you.

7. When others mistreat you, use the RAIN process. This involves mindfully reviewing what has happened to give yourself time to process the experience before you react. Read Ruth King's book, *Mindful of Race* (2018), and use this approach to first care for yourself, and then decide how to respond.

8. Go on a daily walk. If possible, go on a long walk (or run) each day. Be aware of your body. Observe nature. Listen for God. Sometimes, if you have a particular question on your heart, ask the question as you begin your walk and listen for answers as you walk. You might want to take a little notebook along to jot the answers and insights that come.

9. Listen to instrumental music. Music offers an entry into contemplative space and can often calm and soothe a weary or troubled spirit. Try folding clothes to Beethoven, cleaning to Tchaikovsky, or washing dishes with Bach. Lie down on the couch and put on your favorite music and just rest into the sound.

10. Observe art. You can visit a museum, an online gallery, or just sit with a painting or piece of art in your house. Take in the composition meditatively. You might journal about the experience, the various pieces, what you see and learn.

11. Post reminders. Post quotes and reminders to enter contemplative space at key places in your life such as: the dashboard in a car, the corner of a bathroom mirror, the edge of your laptop screen, the surface of your desk, or the coffee table. A few words carefully placed will remind you to enter the contemplative moment.

Suggestions for Group Practice

For a group experience of contemplative living, consider planning a silent retreat. Check with local retreat centers for scheduled retreats or plan a retreat, inviting someone trained in contemplative leadership to lead.

A typical weekend silent retreat begins on Friday night with dinner, followed by an introduction to the theme for the weekend and entering into silence. On Saturday, retreatants may gather in the morning for a session with the retreat leader, but most of the day, they are free to explore and follow the Spirit's leading. Sometimes optional sessions are scheduled for sitting meditation, tea, and/or movement to instrumental music. On Sunday morning, the group gathers to break the silence with a final session and perhaps communion and sharing.

This may seem to be a personal spiritual practice experience and it certainly can be. But this can also be a powerful experience for a group. Sometimes prayer partners are assigned in the opening session, and although you don't talk with each other during the weekend, you do hold each other in prayer. When participating in a silent retreat with a group, there is a strong sense of community coming through the silence. Bonding occurs.

Becoming silent helps cultivate an inner experience of contemplative living. The directions are to follow the Spirit leading. Each person's experience will be different, but generally, it helps a person relax into the now of life, and to walk with God in the moment. This transformative experience can help the pilgrim carry the contemplative approach into their daily life.

Dayspring Retreat Center in Germanton, Maryland, is a silent retreat center, conducting many of these weekend retreats each year. The Shalem Institute for Spiritual Formation conducts training on leading such retreats. They have trained people across the United States, and in South Korea and Canada. A helpful book for leading silent retreats is *Silence, Simplicity and Solitude* (David Cooper, 1992).

An Experience of Contemplative Silence with a Group

If you don't have time for a weekend of silent retreat, you can also plan a shorter time of silence. Even an hour or two in a retreat center or church with options for going outdoors into nature will work. Also, set up a place for art, with supplies to draw, paint, and write. Again, if you have never led a silent retreat, you might find an experienced leader to help with this project.

Introduction. Begin with an introduction to observing silence and answer questions individuals may have. The goal in silent retreat is to be attentive to God and let go of the need to do anything, but rather to be with God. (5 minutes)

Body Prayer. Provide a time of walking mindfully. First have them practice inhaling as they take a step out with their right foot and then exhaling as they step with their left foot. Then lead them in a circle, walking slowly around the room. (5 minutes)

Enter the Silence. Provide a time of silence, depending on whatever time is available.

Provide materials for art and journaling.

Journaling. After the time of silence, when you come back together, begin with a time of personal reflection and journaling with these questions: (10 minutes)

1.   How did the time of mindful walking assist or detract from your presence to your body and God?

2.   What was your experience of silent retreat like for you? How did you spend your time? What was given to you during this time?

3.   Did this help in your awareness of God? Why or why not?

4.   Is this something that you would like to incorporate into your spiritual life on a more regular basis? Why or why not?

Sharing. Provide a time for people to discuss their experiences.

Closing. Close with a prayer.

MULTI-FAITH PERSPECTIVES ON CONTEMPLATIVE PRACTICE

Contemplative practice can bring together people of many different faith traditions. Entering the silence, we let go of dogma and find unity in the heart of God. We come from different understandings, yet we can come together in silence. In this final section of the book, we will explore multi-faith interpretations of meditation and other contemplative practices. I have invited some friends and others who have contemplative spiritual practices to share from their traditions, and I also share of my own Christian practice

Christian – Nancy Flinchbaugh, Author

My contemplative practice. I enjoy the contemplative gifts in this book within my spiritual practice. I begin each day with twenty minutes of meditation and then I journal, beginning with gratitude. My centered actions spring from this early morning time. I meet with a spiritual director regularly and also participate in a monthly circle of spiritual companions. At church, I coordinate quarterly labyrinth walks and walk other labyrinths when possible. Sometimes, I do *Lectio Divina* with scripture or nature as a prelude to my meditation time. When I eat alone, I try mindful eating. I also participate in monthly Taize worship with a group of churches in my community, often playing the violin for these services. As I'm writing this book, I'm starting a new mission group to explore creating a triple bottom line business in my community.

How these practices are part of my religious tradition. The Bible's tapestry contains a central thread of contemplative practice. Clearly, the early Hebrews and Christians practiced silent prayer, the prayer of listening. From the beginning, the Jewish people observed Sabbath, a time of rest. The contemplative practice involves resting in God. God spoke in a still, small voice – a whisper (I Kings 19:9). The early Hebrews learned to hear, by stopping and listening. The Psalmist wrote, "Be still and know that I am God" (Psalm 46:10). The message from the beginning suggests letting go of thoughts and words, sitting with God. The Psalms and other scriptures refer to the natural world, leading to an awareness of God. Silent communion with creation produces inspiration and hope.

And then, we have Jesus, who taught by example. He left the crowds to be alone with God. He prayed on the mountain. He wandered by himself into the desert for three days and nights to listen to God. He rowed out into the water, leaving the people, for silence and communication with his Creator. He taught his followers to go into the closet and pray.

The mystery of the Incarnation reveals Jesus as fully human and fully divine. Followers of Christ are temples of God, aspiring to model his harmony of mind, body, and spirit which contemplative practice reveals. Jesus prayed that all might be one.

In the silence of Christian contemplation, the unity of all creation begins to seep into consciousness and awareness, changing practitioners from deep within, forging a deep connection with transformative love. By returning to a Biblical practice of solitude, being still before God, we can begin to become in touch with our interconnectedness with the Spirit of God alive in creation, and in each of us; the incarnate God.

How this practice helps me personally. In emptying my mind each morning, space for Spirit happens. I believe that I connect with God during this time in a nonverbal way. I believe that I'm presenting myself as a living sacrifice to do God's work, and that's a very joyful experience. The various contemplative practices provide ways for me to listen to God, providing sustenance, illumination and guidance for my journey. Whatever I'm struggling with in my life becomes lighter and transforms in the silence with God. This time becomes my springboard to action. I focus on relationships, my work, my writing. All of them are informed by the silence. I think the practices keep me young and growing and contributing in my life.

What benefit do you see for this practice as part of the larger community in which you live and for the global community? I believe that people who enter the silence are more able to listen and hear others. I believe that people who enter the silence are able to act authentically and in harmony with others. Contemplative practices can reduce the level of violence in our society and also bring us all into deeper connection with the Earth, so that we can answer the call to awaken and care for the earth.

Christian Contemplative (PCUSA) – Therese Taylor-Stinson, Founding Managing Member Spiritual Directors of Color Network, Ltd.

"If you bring forth what is within you, what you bring forth will save you. If you do not bring forth what is within you, what you do not bring forth will destroy you." ~Gospel of Thomas Saying #70

My contemplative practice. My contemplative practice includes Practicing the Presence of God and Centering Prayer. I also live this quote from Lakota Sioux: "Let everything you do be your religion. Let everything you say be your prayer."

How these practices are part of my religious tradition. As I expand in my understanding of being human and living in the Imago Dei, as I elevate my understanding of that most Christians call God, I realize my very life is an act of faith and worship and therefore, not part, but the whole of my religious tradition. In the Presbyterian tradition, this falls into the motto, "Reformed and Always Reforming." (*"ecclesia reformata, semper reformanda"*, meaning the church reformed, always reforming).

My life encourages my deep pondering and being open to Mystery. Christianity was that in the early church, most notably among the desert *ammas* and *abbas* (mothers and fathers). Who were, by the way, most likely people of color.

How this practice helps me personally. It develops my ability to live with uncertainty and to see myself and my actions as part of a larger universal community.

What benefit do you see for this practice as part of the larger community in which you live and for the global community?

The expansion of the beloved community and a living into God's dream.

Muslim/Sufi – Farzana Moon, Writer and Poet

 *My contemplative practice.* I sit on a bed in a comfortable position with my back straight and my feet tucked in under my legs. I try to still my body and empty my mind of all thoughts by concentrating on breathing. I also contemplate the light within my heart with great concentration. Then I feel the subtle breath, which is not just breathing, but divine life energy, sustaining my body, mind and soul.

How these practices are part of my religious tradition. Islam encourages meditation based on the example of Prophet Muhammad's life recorded in Hadiths and verses from the Quran. Below are a couple of Quranic verses and three of Prophet Muhammad's sayings to support the Islamic practice of meditation.

"And do thou O Muhammad remember thy Lord within thyself humbly and with awe, below thy breath at morn and evening. And be not thou of neglectful." Quran (7: 205)

"O thou soul, in complete rest and satisfaction, come back thou to thy Lord. Well pleased and well pleasing to Him. Enter thou then among my devotees, enter thou my Paradise." Quran (89: 27-30)

"Adore God as if you saw Him, for even if you see Him not, He sees you." Hadith Al-Bukhari

"Prophet Muhammad said: one hour of contemplation is better than seven years of worship." Hadith (Suyuti)

"Nine things that my Lord has commanded me: To reverence Him. To speak the truth with propriety, in adversity and prosperity. Moderation in poverty and affluence. Benefit my relatives and kindred who do not

benefit me. Give alms to him who refuses me. Forgive him who injures me. To attain the knowledge of God through silence. Mention God in my heart and speech. I should be an example to God's creatures in love and kindness." Hadith (Tuhuf Al uqool – Short Maxims)

"Once Prophet was sitting in his mosque at Medina and he challenged one of his followers that if he could meditate for five minutes without thinking of any thoughts, he would give him his robe. The follower took the challenges, but after five minutes, when the Prophet asked him if he succeeded, the follower replied: 'almost, but then I started thinking which robe the Prophet would give me?'" Hadith

How this practice helps me personally. It calms my nerves, helps me cope with ailments. It sloughs off any kind of anger, bitterness, or frustration within me. Meditation also makes me perceptive, more loving and forgiving of my own self and others.

What benefit do you see for this practice as part of the larger community in which you live and for global community? It has helped me to be aware of the needy in my community and to help them in any way I can. Also, it has made me aware of the global suffering which I try to alleviate in little ways through my writing. I hope that even if my writing makes a difference in the life of one person, it might achieve universal purpose of living, striving and aspiring toward greater goodwill for the sake of the Whole.

Hindu – Ravi Khanna, Physician

My personal contemplative practice. I follow the eight-step practice of Patanjali: Ashtang Yoga – Raj Yoga. When I was working, I tried to devote one to two hours daily for exercise (mainly walking), Yoga (various Asanas, including Surya Namaskar-Sun salutation, etc.) reading scriptures, and meditation. Since retirement, I have been able to double the above time. I especially try to do Pranayama (breath control) and meditation twice a day. I continue exercise and yoga. Now I have more time to read scripture, especially Hindu philosophy.

The eight step method of Yoga includes 1) Yama, 2) Niyama, 3) Asana (maintaining posture), 4) Pranayama (breathing exercises), 5 Pratyahara (withdrawal of senses), 6) Dharana (concentration), 7) Dhyana (meditation), and 8) samadhi (Realization of oneness with the universe, the true self and liberation).

How this contemplative practice is a part of my religious tradition. In Hinduism, there are various paths to reach the ultimate goal. Raj Yoga is one of the paths, which I follow. They include Shravanam – listening to and reading scripture, Mananam – reflecting upon scripture, and Nidhi Dhayasanam – yoga and meditation.

How this practice benefits me personally. This helps me to find divinity with myself, which is my goal in life. It keeps me peaceful and happy. I find more peace within myself and less irritations and distractions in my mind. I am better able to control my mind and have a positive attitude.

What benefit do you see for this practice as part of the larger community in which you live and for the global community? If I am at peace, others in the community and society may follow a similar path. I now also have additional time for learning about other faiths and working towards increasing peace and harmony, including my participation in the Global Education and Peace Network. The Hindu Dharma teaches me to look at the world as one family and wish for happiness for all.

Buddhist – Debra Williamson, English professor, writer

My personal contemplative practice. I am Buddhist, specifically Tibetan of the Kaygu lineage, of the Mahayana school which aims to relieve the suffering of all beings and bring about their enlightenment by offering one's self in that effort — as differentiated from Theravada which focuses on personal enlightenment. In Mahayana, both lay and monastic Buddhists embrace the four noble truths and the eight-fold path (beliefs and behaviors) toward releasing self and others from samsara, the endless cycle of life, death, and rebirth. Meditation is a significant portion of the Mahayana Buddhist tradition that emphasizes compassionate communication and relationship with others.

My personal meditation or contemplative practice. Before beginning, I light candles around my altar, place fresh water and a food offering there. Sometimes I burn incense as an offering. Then I sit on my cushion on the floor before the altar. Often, I begin by reading about a slogan, belief, or idea. After I finish reading, I say vows and prayers for the enlightenment of all beings, ask to be forgiven for my misdeeds and ignorance, and then dedicate all of these prayers for the benefit and enlightenment of all beings. After dedicating prayers, I practice *tonglen* meditation, a form of *lojong* (mind training) as part of the Shamatha-Vipashyana meditation practice. This training is based on 59 slogans which help us awaken our hearts and to develop compassion for ourselves and others.

How contemplative practice is part of my religious tradition. Meditation is a practice common to Buddhism. Through meditation, we learn to see our patterns of thinking and develop a compassionate approach to ourselves and others. In the *lojong* practice, we learn to be conscious of the ever-flowing thought stream in our minds, to non-judgmentally label them as thoughts, and to release them while we breathe in and out. Treating yourself compassionately is the first step toward developing compassion toward others. Meditation teaches you to befriend yourself, to recognize the deep connections we all have with the pain and suffering of others, and allows you to ventilate your life with compassion.

How my contemplative practice helps me personally. I cultivated this practice because being kind and forgiving to myself was difficult. I often found myself missing in action with others, trapped in the constant pull of my mind stream. I wanted to be present and find some level of peace in my life. I needed to step back and see how the way I was thinking was causing the way I was feeling. Learning meditation taught me that. I began meditation in 1988 at the urgings of my inner voice and during a painful divorce. I continued the practice as I raised my son with special needs. When my oldest son committed suicide nine years ago, the practice deepened as I read The Tibetan Book of the Dead in the 49 days following his death. Each day as I read this book, I felt as if I was journeying though the *bardo*, the space between death and rebirth as I imagined my son, Jason, doing. This practice helped me deal powerfully with grief, and the struggles of everyday life raising Alex, who has severe special needs. I am so grateful to have this practice and what it brings to my everyday life.

What benefit I see for this practice as part of the larger community and for the global community. Being compassionate is essential to building a satisfying life. Many times for me, this means being compassionate to myself when I respond to someone in a way that may feel too direct or unkind. So instead of beating up on myself, telling myself I'm a horrible person because I said something that may have been hurtful, I breathe in and out. I recognize how many people feel this feeling of guilt, or anger, or frustration, and I keep breathing in and out, as a way to drop the story and to feel the energy the emotion brings. I become aware of what I am feeling and I wish that all will be released from suffering, including myself. By doing this, I stop a pattern in my own life and discern how treating myself more kindly allows me to treat others more compassionately as well.

Sikh – Jagdish Singh

What is your religious tradition? Sikh

What is your personal meditation or contemplative practice? In my prayer time, I concentrate on God and the goodness of God. In the Sikh tradition, we believe that God is in everyone, and so I also look into my own self, knowing that I am part of God. Sometimes I meditate on God's face or sing. We believe whatever you feel is okay. I say my prayers in my own mind and God helps me. Whenever I want to feel the peace within me, I reflect in this way. I say my prayers quietly.

How is this a part of your religious tradition? Our religion teaches us to remember God all the time. That's what we are taught and this is what our prayers are like. We get up on the morning and say our prayers. Or even if we are doing mundane tasks, we can say our prayers, remembering God is really important.

How does this practice help you personally? It helps me if I have problems. I'll read our holy book with the words, or I listen to the words, and it helps me. Praying and singing helps me. When I do this, I realize that whatever happens, I have to accept what's going on. Sometimes it's not always easy to accept things, but I believe this is God's will.

What benefit do you see for this practice as part of the larger community in which you live and for the global community? The community is very important to us and prayers do help.

CENTERED ACTION

Sitting into Hopeful Action

I am learning to sit

as I work for peace.

I am learning to value silence

as I organize for justice.

I am learning to listen to all of Creation

as I speak for the Earth.

In sitting, I encounter joy

dancing into playful interconnections.

In silence, I discover possibilities

deepening into transformative relationships.

In hearing, I realize miracles

awakening into hopeful action.

On Centered Action

"The true contemplative is not less interested than others in normal life, not less concerned with what goes on in the world, but more interested, more concerned. The fact that he or she is a contemplative makes them capable of a greater interest and a deeper concern. The contemplative has the inestimable gift of appreciating at their real worth values that are permanent, authentically deep, human, truly spiritual, and even divine. Their mission is to be a complete and whole person, with an instinctive and generous need to further the same wholeness in others, and in all humanity. They arrive at this, however, not by superior gifts and talents, but by the simplicity and poverty which are essential to their state because these alone keep one traveling in the way that is spiritual, divine and beyond understanding." – Thomas Merton [19]

"Everybody can be great... because anybody can serve. You don't have to have a college degree to serve. You don't have to make your subject and verb agree to serve. You only need a heart full of grace. A soul generated by love." Martin Luther King, Jr.

In this busy, crazy life we struggle to find time to relax. Perhaps for this reason, the contemplative approach becomes so crucial to our peace of mind. This book offers many ways to carve that silence into every day. Learning to slow down, to listen, to be mindful, and to meditate, provides a counterbalance to the frenetic tendencies of our society. Hearing that still small voice makes a big difference to us now. In former times, silence happened in almost every moment. Now, it's the exception, something that needs to be sought and cultivated.

Our contemplative practice helps us center into the love of the

---

[19] *The Sign of Jonas* by Thomas Merton, New York City, New York: Harcourt, Brace & Co., N.Y. 1953, pp. 69.

Creator. We focus our lives so that we can live and move from our heart centers. But it's not enough to sit into silence, to walk the labyrinth, to eat mindfully, and to listen to the Earth and scripture. No, it's not enough. We are also called to love. We must listen for our calling. We must find ways to use our gifts. We must act out of the passion of our hearts to love and create a better world.

Barbara Holmes explains, "Activism and contemplation are not functional opposites. Rather contemplative spirituality, is at its heart, a reflective activity always seeking a spiritual balance between individual piety and community justice seeking." She asserts that the great justice movements of the twentieth century came from "consistent contemplative practices of those seeking liberation." Both passive resistance and active protests leading to the civil rights movement came from this center. (*Joy Unspeakable*. 2017, p. 113).

Our action is so important. As humans, we are the consciousness of Earth. We are the intelligent beings that have the power to love and create or hate and destroy. The Christian scripture clearly calls us to love and to act on behalf of the least of us. Clearly, from the beginning, Jesus taught the two most important commandments: loving God and loving others (Luke 10:27, Mark 12:29-31). The time communing with God provides a wellspring which leads into loving others. Jesus offered living water to all who believe in him (John 4:13-15).

Shalem founder Tilden Edwards,[20] beautifully describes this wellspring in a lecture at a Shalem Society Annual Gathering (October 2012). "In the silence, the Christian encounters the radiant presence of God, the overflowing energy of love which ignites sparks, leaping into flames of hope, fueled by mutual

---

[20] Tilden Edwards is an Episcopal priest and the founder of Shalem Institute for Spiritual Formation in Washington, DC. What follows summarizes a presentation he delivered in October 2012 at the Annual Gathering of Shalem Associates.

indwelling love. Burning hope cascades into mind, shaping visions of what can be: possibilities, plans of how to overcome." At this point, he said, "the mind passes the baton to the ego where mindful action works out unique embodiment. And there in the grassroots, movement springs into courageous action."

The contemplative life, therefore, takes the Christian out into the world in courageous action, rooted and deeply connected to the love of God, nourished by a deep spring of living water. As we take time to draw near to the Heart of God, we will be spurred to action. And we must work together, as the great prophet Thomas Berry once said. "We will go together as a single sacred community or we will all perish in the desert."[21] This is our great work.

What are the actions that are needed in this time? Finding a new way to care for our Earth, addressing climate change, forging a sustainable path into the future, and other good environmental practices are so important. Also, we must find better ways to care for people, address racism, feed the hungry, and shape governments that take positive actions on behalf of all. There is so much to be done.

---

[21] Thomas Berry. *The Dream of the Earth*, Oakland, California: Sierra Club Books, 1988, p. 35.

A Letter from the Earth on Contemplative Action 1/21/19

Dear One,

Your actions in this world are extensions of your love. When you sit into silence and let Me enter your consciousness, you do my work in your day. I know it may be hard for you to fathom that this is real, but it is. Each time you perform an act of kindness, when you organize to care for the Earth, when you act with love out of your center, you do it for Me and fulfill all my hopes for the creation.

If everyone tuned in to Me each day, this world would be a different place. There would be no killing. There would be more bona fide community. You would find ways of turning around climate change.

So, Dear One, be persistent. Be hard-working. But always, temper doing with being. Take care for the quality of your work. May it evolve from your heart center where you connect with Me each day.

Even in the darkest nights, keep the candle burning. Consider your love opportunities.

You do not walk alone. I am with you always.

Love, Gaia.

Nancy's Thoughts on Contemplative Action

How then shall we live? Our human journeys provide so many choices. For me, beginning at a young age, I dedicated my life to serve God and people. That keeps me busy. Over time, my mission developed to include working for peace, justice, and the Earth. Yes, I've been very busy in my life. But good actions can quickly become empty and devoid of love. Hard work exhausts the mind, body and spirit. Giving oneself in service becomes very difficult when there is no inner well. Likewise, spiritual practice can become an empty experience, when it doesn't lead into loving action.

I've stayed close to the church throughout my life, and I always try to find a church that knows how to wed the journey of the Spirit and the life of loving action. Sometimes it seems to me that church people don't address the cries of the poor and victims of injustice enough. I left the church in my twenties with my own brand of righteous anger for a while and enrolled in law school to solve the problems. Although a good career for many, I didn't enjoy the legal approach to life. When I turned back to God, I began to draw from the contemplative well from which my future actions would spring.

Over time, I've found that I need both spiritual practice and action. And since I've begun my meditation practice, I've found my actions flowing much more easily throughout the days and weeks of my life. Certainly, there are still challenges, but I do really believe that I find direction from the still small voice that emerges from the solitude.

When I received this letter from Gaia on contemplative action, I felt so happy. It's wonderful to know that I am truly in sync with the Creator when I'm seeking her in silence each morning. I'm so glad there is a path to overcome the injustices, the violence, the destruction of the Earth by allowing God to live through us.

Gaia's so hopeful. Do you hear her voice calling you, too? I've been receiving these letters for several years now, and I think that hope is what springs into me when I receive a letter. She's right, when we come together in community, we can accomplish great things.

For many years, I've had a deep interest in career counseling. I believe that part of each person's journey on earth is to discover their unique gifts and passions, to develop them and live them out in their daily lives. I love this quote, "The place God calls you to is the place where your deep gladness and the world's deep hunger meet." (Frederick Buechner, *Wishful Thinking: A Theological ABC*, 1993).[22]

One time, a friend and I led a small group in our church for people wanting to discern their calling. We met for 10 weeks. During the first few weeks, we completed a series of exercises that career counselors might assign their clients. We explored what we enjoy doing and

Facilitating a meeting: The Global Education and Peace Network

passions. We wrote fantasies of what we'd like to do with our lives. We completed interest and skill inventories. And then we

---

[22]Frederick Buechner, *Wishful Thinking: A Seeker's ABC*, San Francisco, California: HarperOne, 1993, (p. 118-119),

wrote a summary of what we learned. After we completed the various exercises, we provided a copy of our learning for each person in the group. For the next several weeks, we prayed for each other and focused on each member one at a time, offering discernment and support. A couple women in that group felt a call to ministry, and later attended seminary. I expressed my call to work for peace and justice, which I believed to be extremely unpractical. I still remember my pastor telling me that night, "Nancy, things have a way of working out, if that's your call." Much to my surprise, as I continued my focus on that path, a few years later, I was hired to work as a fair housing and mediation coordinator in local government. Thus, I continued to do peace and justice work for many years, while supporting my family and following my call. One of the joys of my job involves facilitating a Global Education and Peace Network, working to bring intercultural programs and an annual calendar to the community.

Several years ago in our community, a neighborhood organizer brought Asset-Based Community Development to town. As they sought to turn our most impoverished elementary school into a Promise School, they worked in the neighborhood to help the people find ways to utilize their skills and talents (assets) around areas of their passion to address the challenges in their neighborhood. Instead of a top-down, needs assessment approach, bringing in people to solve the problems of the neighborhood, the approach suggests that you build on the strengths of the people already in the neighborhood. They even invited me to lead a contemplative small group in the midst of their work.

Today, there is a community vegetable garden, where once was a vacant lot. The garden is tended by neighbors. The produce provides nutritious food for them. Over time, they also extended the gardening projects into individual backyards. Some of the produce is sold on neighborhood vegetable stands. That has spurred other community gardens and gardens by the elementary schools. I think that's a good model for all of us as we seek to live out love in our world.

My husband, in his younger days, lived in Washington, D.C. Beginning in the 1940s, a small church developed, exploring a new model to wed the contemplative life with the life of action, called Church of the Savior, led by Gordon Cosby. My husband participated in this church in his young adulthood. In this church, everyone was expected to join a mission group. The mission groups emerged from the parent church around areas of common calling. Each mission group not only engaged in a project, but also helped provide accountability to each member to maintain a spiritual practice. So many creative ministries have been spawned from this nucleus. A housing ministry, a ministry of money, a caring house for people whose bodies were failing, a ministry of prayer and intercession for the government, a ministry for re-entering citizens, a contemplative retreat center, an experimental environmental community. In later years, they disbanded the original church. While many still mourn the loss of the main body, the leaders believe that the mission groups are the church. Maintaining the original church drew too much energy work from the work of the church in mission. Now, new groups sometimes emerge from existing mission groups. I find this to be an excellent model for moving love into action within a centered community. You can read about their many ministries on their website at inwardoutward.org.

There is much to be done, and we each must find our path. My life has taken me into peacemaking. I've been a mediator and taught conflict resolutions skills. My life calls me to work for social justice. I've worked in fair housing for many years. I coordinate intercultural programming, working to build bridges among people and more understanding.

I also work for the Earth. The Citizens' Climate Lobby, I believe, is an amazing group of over 100,000 people now, working to build political will to address climate change. This, for me, is the most crucial work in our time. I continue to listen to how I can contribute and be involved with them as we write letters, meet with congressional representatives and speak up for our recommended solution of a revenue-neutral fee and dividend on the fossil fuels, to allow the market to naturally develop alternative fuels, thereby reducing carbon emissions. Check us out at: citizensclimatelobby.org.

I hope that you will find your path and your responsible journey into love as you sit into silence. I do believe that both are so important. And for this reason, I've also added another part to my life mission. Beyond serving God and people, in addition to working for peace, justice and the Earth, I also strive to be a contemplative evangelist!

Suggestions for Personal Practice

1. Spend time listening and discerning your own mission in life. There are many resources that can help you. I highly recommend the book *What Color is Your Parachute* by Richard Bolles.[23] This book has a section in the back on discovering your life mission. But also, it helps you figure out what exactly you want to be doing and with whom. Another helpful resource, if you are thinking about retirement is Marjorie Zoet Bankston's book, *Creative Aging: Rethinking Retirement and Non-Retirement in a Changing World* (2010).[24]

2. Take time to identify your passions and make sure that your mission revolves around your passion. You will be much more effective working about things that concern you, rather than doing things others want you to do.

3. Set goals around your mission and ask for help as you sit into silence each day. We have so much personal power in our lives to accomplish great things, but it all begins with being clear and focused. The power of intention is so important. Have you heard the thought, "If you don't know where you're going, you'll end up somewhere else."? Intentional living takes you where you want to go.

4. Take time out for retreat days to refocus and refresh yourself.

5. Get out and explore and find others who are working on projects that are important to you. You can accomplish so much more with others. Join their efforts.

---

[23] Richard Bolles, *What Color is Your Parachute*. Ten Speed Press, Revised, 2019.

[24] Marjorie Zoet Bankston. Creative Aging: Rethinking Retirement and Non-Retirement in a Changing World. Nashville, Tennessee: Skylight Paths, 2010.

6. If you feel a strong call to do a project and can't find others doing what you want to do, invite others in your religious community or community at large and bring them together to consider how to move forward. See the Mission Group strategy below to get started.

Suggestions for a Group Process to Listen for Mission/Action

Introduction. Begin with an introduction to contemplative action. (5 minutes)

Body Prayer. Guided meditation on the body, focusing and relaxing each part and guiding awareness of the body functioning as a whole. See suggested script on Page 209. (5 minutes).

Silence. Introduce a time of silence. (5 minutes)

Considering Mission/Action. Give each person a sheet with the following prompts (20 minutes)

Do you feel a sense of call from God to action in your life? If so, what is your call?

What are the ways you serve others in your life?

What are your passions?

What are your gifts?

What would you say is your life mission?

Do you think you are already using your gifts and talents around your area of passion? If not, is there anything you would like to consider exploring?

Is there any training or experience you would like to acquire to help you toward your call/mission?

Silent Writing/Drawing. Continue with a time of silent writing, doodling and/or drawing, reflecting on the time. Instrumental music may be played in the background. (10 minutes)

Reflection. Reflect and/or journal on the following:

1. How was your experience of body prayer? In what ways did that help or not help your awareness of God within you?

2. What was your experience of considering life mission, actions,

gifts and service? In what ways was this helpful to you? Were there any problems for you in thinking about this?

3. How did the time of journaling and/or drawing assist in your consideration of action?

Group Sharing. Provide time for the group to share observations, experiences.   (5-10 minutes)

Closing. Ask each person to share something they feel called to do or a way they serve others. (5 minutes)

Group Response: We ask for God to bless your service of: Repeat the call/service each will do.

Body Prayer: Guided Relaxation

A suggested script for a guided meditation to heighten relaxation and awareness of the body, leading into a time of a silent meal and mindful eating.

Begin by encouraging everyone to get into a comfortable position. Invite people to lie on the floor (if appropriate to your setting) and if not, to sit in a comfortable position, feet resting on the floor. Script: Now, I'm going to guide you in a process of relaxation. Close your eyes and take a few deep breaths... in... and out...in... and out... in... and out... Now, as you breathe in, tighten all the muscles in your feet and toes. As you breathe out, relax your feet and toes. It is now their rest time. Now as you breathe in, tighten all the muscles in your thighs and lower legs down to your ankles. Good. Now as you breathe out, relax all of these muscles and just let them sink down, supported by the floor. Now as you breathe in, tighten all the muscles in your abdomen and hips. Then breathe out, releasing them and telling them it is now their rest time. Good. Now, as you breathe in, tighten all the muscles in your chest, shoulders, arms, and hands, scrunch them tight together and hold for a moment, then breathe out and let them rest. Feel your body at peace, relaxed from your shoulders all the way down to your toes. Good. Now, breathe in and tighten your neck and head, scrunch up your face and make a grimace. Hold that for a second and then breathe out and let it go. Feel your entire body at peace, relaxed and happy. Sit for a few moments, just observing your breath, sinking down into the Earth, letting it support you, giving your whole body a rest in gratitude for the work it performs for you each day. (pause). When you're ready, open your eyes. Stretch and come back to our group.

Suggestion for a Mission Group

And so, we reach the end of this brief dip into the contemplative life. I would like to leave this book open-ended, for both you and for me. As I write this morning, I'm thinking about a call to mission that I've had for several years now. I heard a call to start a triple bottom line business to develop alternative energy for my community and beyond. A triple bottom line business not only tries to make Profit, but also takes into consideration the People and the Planet in everything they do. And so I'm ending this book with a challenge to myself to assemble a mission group to begin this business. I'm going to be inspired by my friends at the Church of the Savior in Washington, D.C., on how to start. They've started many mission projects, still thriving. Perhaps this is the culmination of my own journey inward, that I solidify an outward project working in the culmination. Perhaps you will hear a call and begin with me, as a conclusion to this book. We've only just begun.

**Triple Bottom Line
"TBL" LENT MISSION GROUP**

· **Committing to Spiritual Discipline during Lent.**
· **Connecting for weekly meals and sharing/prayer**
· **Listening for Call**
· **Exploring possibilities**

ARE YOU READY FOR ADVENTURE? DO YOU WANT TO EXPLORE WITH US AND LISTEN TO GOD AND EACH OTHER? If so, join us...

**Kick-off: Mardis Gras Potluck Meal and Meeting
Tuesday, March 5, 5:30-7:00 p.m. at First Baptist
638 S. Fountain.**
Continuing: The Sundays of Lent 5-7 pm with potluck meals at the Flinchbaugh-Schlather Home, 1402 St. Paris Road on March 10, 17, 24 (Taize at First Lutheran), 31, April 7, 14, 21.

Invitation to a group that I held during Lent 2019

END MATTERS

Trust

Some days life overwhelms me --

The cries of the poor,

The cries of the rich,

I cry trying to mediate it all.

Some days responsibilities pull --

I work on one project;

I work on another;

I'm torn among so many important priorities.

Some days, I can't figure it out --

The amazing goodness and potential, the miraculous nature of life;

The disturbing evils, planet and family destruction, greed, violence;

I do so little.

So I'm learning to sit --

Eclipsing all the good into the silent spaciousness of God;

Letting all the evil go into oblivion;

Merging self into sacred space, unity.

And then I take that unity, peace, wholeness –

Back into the wonderful mysteries of this day;

Back into the trying circumstances of my life;

Trusting God, letting the Loving Spirit lead.

Finger Walking the Living Vine Labyrinth

Nancy's Closing Thoughts

As we come to the end of this brief primer on contemplative practices, I want to say a few final words. I began this primer while leading a retreat several years ago. I continued to work on it as a resource for both myself and others to guide people into the richness of the silence and the contemplative life, close to the heart of God. I hope you will find some tools helpful for you in both your personal contemplative journey and your communal contemplative forays. I've used many of the sections as handouts in whole or in part for leading short sessions in my church and other workshops I've offered. I encourage you to do likewise.

I've offered some bibliographical references, limiting them to books that have been helpful to me on my own contemplative path. I know there are so many more resources that are also available. I encourage you to explore, seek, and find more.

This morning, as I searched for words to close this little primer, I found myself walking my Living Vine Finger Labyrinth to listen. The Living Vine Labyrinth we made at our church has the colors of the chakras painted in flowers at each turn. My home finger labyrinth replicates the one at our church, but was designed on a 12 inch square canvas, paper mâché over thick twine and painted with acrylics.

As my fingers walked into the labyrinth, they first encountered the purple flowers, a symbol of the royal crown chakra, signifying connection with divinity. Yes, I thought. First and foremost, the contemplative practices draw us deeper into communion with God, the Spiriting force of love at the center of all life.

Next, I encountered the indigo flowers, signifying the third eye of intuition. As we slow down and listen in contemplative practices, we are able to hear not only God, but also our own intuitive knowing that helps guide us onto our unique path. Therein lies both our passion and joy and we receive the guidance to navigate the challenges of each day.

Then, my finger moved into the light blue flower, a symbol for the throat chakra, and I reminisced on how often I've found my voice in my times of silence and contemplative journaling. I find the words needed in my life and, from my center, I write. I craft speeches in the sacred time after my meditation practice.

At the fourth chakra, the central one, I encountered the green flower which stands for the heart center, love. And I know that it is here in the silence that I also come in contact with my heart and the love, which is the very essence of our Creator. From this center, I can move out into my life, empowered to love the people in my life, and also myself, with that unconditional love of God, that Love who teaches and caresses me in the silence.

Taking heart, I arrived at the gold flower of courage, the solar plexus chakra. So often, I find courage in the silence to do the important work of my life. And somehow, with my daily practice, the work becomes easier and less of a strain, after gaining the strength of the Spirit.

And then, my finger danced on and into the orange flower of womb and reproductive organs, where creativity blooms. I do believe that as we dwell closer to the heart of God, we long to create with our Creator. And then after our contemplative practice, we find inspiration to dance into the creative solutions needed in these challenging times in which we live.

Finally, my finger came home to the red flower, the root chakra, where I also find my true self, near the center of the labyrinth where I am loved by God. Here, I can imagine myself putting my own roots deep into the good earth and branching into the unique child of God that I am called and created to be.

As my finger completed the walk, it passed on into the center of the labyrinth, where I rested with the flowers, the purple, indigo, blue, green, gold, orange and red flowers, all growing out of a single seed. Here, I feel the completion of my journey, finding my rest in the heart of God, from which I will continue to move and have my being.

After a time of prayer, my finger began its way back out, and I knew then a sense of completion. The book is ready to go out with me, into the world, to teach and instruct and lead others home into the Heart of God.

I close with a prayer that this little primer will be a blessing to you on journey, as it has been on mine. Sending blessings on you and your journey with love,

Nancy Flinchbaugh, Springfield, Ohio 1/23/20

About the Living Vine Labyrinth

by Nancy Flinchbaugh.

First Baptist Church, 638 South Fountain Ave., Springfield, Ohio

Our church's labyrinth journey began in July 2005, when several congregational members designed a backyard grass labyrinth for my 50th birthday. They presented me with a purple boa, a red hat, and showed me the way to the path. Several friends began to journey to Dayton's labyrinth at Westminster Presbyterian Church. I thought we needed one in Springfield.

Five years later one of the labyrinth makers turned 60, and I wanted to return the favor by making a cloth labyrinth for her. The year came and went, but the following year when our worship team planned five services in July and August of 2011, the final service scripture focused on a contemplative Jesus climbing the mountain to pray. We planned a contemplative Taize service and decided it would be the perfect time to introduce a labyrinth to our congregation and celebrate our friend's 61st birthday.

When we journey with God, the sacred path often unfolds in mysterious and wonderful ways, and so did ours. The creation of the labyrinth involved community, friendship, faith, hope, love and perseverance. When we finally began, we had two weeks – but with God, all things are possible.

My good friend, Holly Wolfe, took to the internet and soon lifted up possibilities and designs. In the midst of a torrential downpour one July evening, she met me at Lowe's after work to look at drop cloths that we thought could become a labyrinth. A week later, I purchased four 9 X 12 canvas drop cloths and three 6 X 9 cloths with Holly's blessing, and the labyrinth creation began.

I quickly realized that sewing these drop cloths together was a bit beyond my abilities and I began to email church friends and call tent makers in the community. A few days later at a funeral no less, Mary Jane Salyers, aka saint in my book, offered to sew it together over the weekend. I dropped off the drop cloths on Thursday night and on Sunday morning her husband, Bill Salyers, carried the now unified drop cloths into our church basement and my elation hit the roof until Holly and I began to try to figure out how to draw the labyrinth onto the cloth. We met several nights, after she got off work at her second job and argued and calculated, until I came up with a string, attached to a bolt in the center, which Holly held steady while I circled the cloth with my pencil also attached to a string. At first, our knees became scratched and torn. Holly asked me to provide her with knee pads and then asked if I could circle while standing and bending over. It worked swimmingly and "Voila!" within one evening we had 8 concentric circles and the labyrinth was easily finished from there.

We chose the Santa Rosa Labyrinth pattern (http://www.srlabyrinthfoundation.com), which Holly particularly liked. Because we were limited in space in our church fellowship hall, we decided on a seven-circuit pattern. The design is copyrighted, but we weren't really planning to profit from our venture and Holly's research suggested we were permitted to use the copyrighted design if we were using it without profit. Then as I began to research paints, I quickly decided that perhaps magic markers would work a little easier. And somehow, in my growing Eco Spirituality focus, I had conceived the possibility of making our labyrinth out of green vines. You can imagine my delight when I found 14 wide green Sharpie markers at Office Max.

Our birthday friend, Debbie Copeland, came the night we designed the vine, making a perfect leaf pattern. Then Holly created the pattern for laying out the leaves and with a little more fine tuning, we were off, drawing and coloring vines on our 23 foot labyrinth. I bought clamps and we strung together 8-foot-long tables to create a surface to work, and even bought PVC pipe on which to roll the cloth as we worked. Along with our plant theme, I thought some flowers at the turns would be nice and enlisted our church artist, Amy Woodburn. She developed a wonderful, simple design and dropped them off, during her 4-H County Fair week. I had been impressed with rainbow labyrinths, so we added this to the flower concept. As you walk into the labyrinth, you begin with the purple and move through the rainbow, or chakras if you prefer, down to the red or root as you move into the circle; and then from the root to the head as you move out.

Another miraculous aspect of the creation came in the many people who pitched in to help and the amazing reality that two weeks later, we actually had the labyrinth complete and ready for prayer. Several of us began to walk it and slowly a Labyrinth Walkers Group formed that met in October for a time of blessing the labyrinth and planning for the future. We began to open it to the community, with three openings during the Christmas season, which became wonderful Friday night Meditative Happy Hours, twice with a live harpist.

You will notice that our labyrinth is not perfect. One of the 6 X 9 cloths is a different fabric and size. From the beginning, I believed the imperfections were an important part of the labyrinth. The larger cloth turned out to be a place for putting on socks and prayer before the walk. We extended the vine over one of the paths and had to paint a correction, a reminder of life's bumps. Most recently, some ash from a match spilled on the cloth and in cleaning it off, we further soiled the cloth. And now, one of our group members, Kathy Whitt, has a plan to make the blemishes yet another blessing by enlisting our church artist to devise a way to stencil the path with a stone-like design, so that the labyrinth will continue to grow and deepen with use.

The labyrinth has become a center for contemplative practice at our church. At first, we held meditative walks on the first Friday of every month. Now we hold quarterly walks on Saturday mornings. The labyrinth has helped draw in people seeking a contemplative journey, as well as provided a place for the contemplatives in our church to gather, love each other and dream together about how God is leading us as we continue to circle into God and our lives.

You may follow our labyrinth on Facebook at: http://www.facebook.com/pages/Living-Vine-Labyrinth/274196749285914. For more information or to arrange a session for your group, you may call the church office at (937) 325-5537.

How to Make an Appreciation Book

What is An Appreciation Book? An appreciation book is a collection of photos and comments from multiple people to encourage and appreciate someone going through a major transition, celebrating a milestone or facing an illness. Graduations, milestone birthdays, retirements, facing surgery, or even a terminal illness can be good times for such a book. What follows are suggestions for designing the book:

1.   Design a response sheet. Design a sheet to make it easy for people to respond and contribute. At the top, include a brief sentence about why you are doing the book and how you'll include their thoughts and provide information and how they can submit their information and when. Here's an example I used when my friend, Tiffany Wanzo, was graduating from college:

Top of sheet: *On January 7, we are having a college graduation party for Tiffany. For the party, we are making her a little book. You can participate, if you wish, by completing this form. Complete some or all of these prompts, and we will include your thoughts in the book. If you have a photo you'd like to attach of you and/or your family, please do. Please return it to me by Friday, January 6. Email, mail, drop it off, call or text!*

Congratulations, Tiffany! What I want to celebrate about you is…

Thank you, Tiffany, for….

My prayer for you is…

My wish for you is…

Any other comments…

2.   Create a Publisher greeting card document. As I begin to receive the responses, I create a Publisher document, a quarter-fold card. You can find this under "blank page" layout designs. When you open a new document, choose "more blank page sizes" and scroll down to "Greeting Cards". I usually choose the "1/4 Letter

Side Fold 5.5 x 4.5". Use Word Art to add the prompt to each page, then make a text box on each page to add the responses. This way, you can type in the responses on single sheets, saving them as separate files, ready to print out. Make sure you put the name of the person who wrote the response on the bottom of each sheet, because you'll later cut these sheets up and put them in different parts of the book. Also, make sure your margins allow you to trim off an inch on the 4.5 inch height, to fit into the 4x6" photo slots in the album. Another option is to actually print out the Publisher page and people can hand-write their response onto the page. Or you could also email the publisher file and those with Publisher can just type their responses into the document.

3.   Search social media. If people don't send photos, search social media for photos to use. Facebook friends offer many possibilities of themselves to use. You can easily click on the photo and choose "save as", downloading photos for use, if you don't have them in your personal collection.

5.   Purchase a photo album. Purchase a photo album that takes 4" x 6" horizontal photos, making sure you'll have enough room. Usually a 100 or 200 photos book is enough. Try to estimate how much room you'll need. Say you have 20 responses, that might be 80 sheets of response and 20 photos, which would be 100.

6.   Assemble the album. Wait until you have most of the responses before assembling the book. Then I like to do a section in the book for each of the prompts, putting all the responses of the same prompt together. So for the example above, I'd start with all the "Congratulations" comments, then the "Thank you" and so on. Or you could put all the comments from one person together and then move on to the next person. Cut the publisher sheets into four little sheets. When you cut the individual sheets, keep in mind they must fit into a 4x6 inch slot. The 5.5" length will be fine, but you have 4.5" height that will need to be trimmed. So, make sure you leave margins when typing, and then trim off at least a quarter

inch from the top and bottom, to make them fit. Put photos of the individuals who responded next to their responses in the book. You might have multiple pictures of one person, but if not, at least put a photo by one of their responses.

7.   Add event photos later. If you do have a party or event, you might leave room to put pictures from the party at the back of the book. Also, you can print out blank sheets with the prompts and have them on a table, giving a chance for those who didn't contribute to the book to be added. This way, the book becomes not only an expression of gratitude, but also a nice memory of the special event. (For Tiffany, I included pictures of her graduation in the book.)

8.   Plan for originality. Sometimes people don't want to use the prompts or they want to respond in another way. You can always scan or take a picture of the response when they don't fit into the 4x6" slot and shrink them, printing them out to fit. Or you might include an envelope with additional responses that don't fit into the album. While most people go along with this request, I've found some prefer to write a card and do a private message to the individual.

Choosing Scripture Passages for Lectio Divina

When entering into a time of Lectio Divina, you must select a short passage of scripture. A simple way to do this would be to use the lectionary texts for the Sunday of the week. A good resource for this is the Vanderbilt website at: https://lectionary.library.vanderbilt.edu/. If you are focusing on a particular theme, you could do an online search for scripture references on your topic. You might want to avoid long narrative passages and focus on passages with kernels of faith and truth. Many of the Psalms lend themselves well to *Lectio Divina*. Some of the scriptures that I have enjoyed using are Psalm 23, Psalm 139 and Philippians 4.

Thelma Hall's, *Too Deep for Words: Rediscovering Lectio Divina* (1988), includes instructions for traditional *Lectio Divina* and its theological background but also includes a guide to scripture organized by 50 themes, with references for 500 different scripture texts that could be used.

Directions for Making Earth Prayer Beads

Sheet created by Nancy Flinchbaugh, 2012. Based on a project introduced by Barbara Davis, Spirituality Network of Columbus, Ohio.
Use freely to promote praying for the earth and our role as stewards thereof!

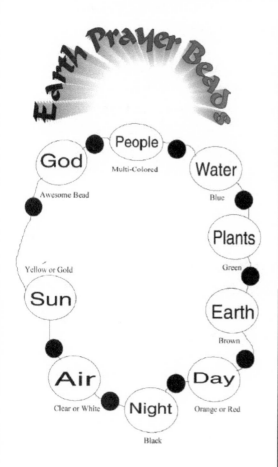

Make Your Prayer Beads...

1. Select Prayer Beads.
2. String your Prayer Beads with a little bead between each bigger bead.
3. Tie your elastic. Glue the knot to keep it secure.

Use Your Prayer Beads each day to pray for the earth and your role in it...
    Start with the God Bead, giving thanks to God for all of creation. Then pray for the people of the earth; and for your role in caring for the earth; then give thanks and contemplate the water, plants, earth, day, night, air, sun.
    Let the colors remind you of the many-colored wonders of God's creation.

About Shalem Institute for Spiritual Formation

For excellent training and support on your contemplative path, I highly recommend the Shalem Institute for Spiritual Formation. Here is how they describe themselves on their website at shalem.org.

"Since 1973, the Shalem Institute for Spiritual Formation has fostered contemplative living and leadership by caring for the spiritual heart in prayer and by offering ways of opening into the life of the Spirit through our programs and other resources. We welcome individuals wherever they are on the path of spiritual discovery.

Shalem is grounded in Christian contemplative spirituality yet draws on the wisdom of many religious traditions. We provide opportunity for spiritual exploration individually and within a community of seekers.

Our partnerships with like-minded organizations enable Shalem's ministry to expand around the world. Shalem is one of the most respected centers for spiritual deepening in the US and globally.

We provide resources for contemplative living, prayerful reading, invitations to silence, retreat weekends, online courses, speakers and events, and long-term programs for clergy seeking to go deeper, aspiring spiritual directors, contemplative retreat and prayer group leaders, and executives seeking to lead from the heart."

Find more information on their website at shalem.org.

Bibliography

Meditation

Edwards, Tilden. *Living in the Presence: Disciplines for the Spiritual Heart*. San Francisco, California: Harper & Row, 1995.

Finley, James. *Christian Meditation: Experiencing the Presence of God*. San Francisco, California: Harper, 2004.

Keating, Thomas. *Open Mind, Open Heart*. New York City, New York: Amity House, 1986.

Koch, Carl and Joyce Heil. *Created in God's Image: Meditating on our Body*. Winona, Minnesota: St. Mary's Press, 1991.

Laird, Martin. *Into the Silent Land: A Guide to the Christian Practice of Contemplation*. New York City, New York: Oxford University Press, 2006.

McColman, Carl. *Befriending Silence*. Notre Dame, Indiana: Ave Maria Press, 2015.

Ryan, Thomas, editor. *Reclaiming the Body in Christian Spirituality*. Mahway, New Jersey: Paulist Press, 2004.

Ryan, Thomas. *Prayer of Heart and Body: Meditation and Yoga as Christian Spiritual Practice*. Mahwah, New Jersey: Paulist Press 1995.

Teresa of Avila (author) with Mirabai Starr (translator). *Interior Castle*. New York City, New York: Riverhead Books, 2004.

Thich Nhat Hanh, *The Wisdom of Thich Nhat Hanh*. New York: One Spirit, 2000.

Wolpert, Daniel. *Creating a Life with God: The Call of Ancient Prayer Practices*. Nashville, Tennessee: Upper Room: 2003.

Labyrinth Walk

Artress, Lauren. *Walking a Sacred Path: Rediscovering the Labyrinth as Sacred Practice*. New York City, New York: Riverhead Books, 2006.

Artress, Lauren. *The Sacred Companion: A Guide to Walking the Labyrinth to Heal and Transform*. New York City, New York:

Riverhead Books, 2006.

Schaper, Donna and Carol Ann Camp. *Labyrinths from the Outside In (2nd Edition): Walking to Spiritual Insight—A Beginner's Guide (Walking Together, Finding the Way)*. Woodstock, Vermont: Skylight Paths, 2013.

Villemaire, Lorraine. *The Labyrinth Experience: An Educator's Resource*. Independently published, 2019.

Sacred Conversation

Adesanya, Ineda Pearl (editor), *Kaleidoscope: Broadening the Palette in the Art of Spiritual Direction*, New York City, New York: Church Publishing Inc, 2019.

Bryant-Johnson, Sherry, Therese Taylor-Stinson and Rosalie Norman-McNaney (Editors), *Embodied Spirits: Stories of Spiritual Directors of Color*, New York City, New York: Morehouse Publishing, 2013.

Edwards, Tilden. *Spiritual Director, Spiritual Companion. Guide to Tending the Soul*. Mahwah, New Jersey: Paulist Press, 2001.

Edwards, Tilden. *Spiritual Friend: Reclaiming the Gift of Spiritual Direction*. Mahwah, New Jersey: Paulist Press, 1979.

Fryling, Alice. *Seeking God Together: An Introduction to Group Spiritual Direction*, Westmont, Illinois: IVP Books, 2008.

Guenther, Margaret. *Holy Listening: The Art of Spiritual Direction*. Boston, Massachusetts: Cowley Publications, 1992.

Kelsey, Morton. *Companions On The Inner Way: The Art of Spiritual Guidance*. Hertford, North Carolina: Crossroad Press, 1995.

Taylor-Stinson, Therese (editor). *Ain't Gonna Let Nobody Turn Me Around: Stories of Contemplation and Justice*. New York City, New York: Church Publishing Inc, 2017.

To locate spiritual directors: Visit the Spiritual Directors of Color Network Directory (http://sdcnetwork.org/sdn-directory/) and the Spiritual Directors International "Seek and Find Guide" (https://www.sdiworld.org/find-a-spiritual-director/seek-and-find-guide)

Gratitude Practice

Ban Breathnach, Sarah. *Simple Abundance: A Daybook of Comfort and Joy.* New York City, New York: Grand Central Publishing, 1997.
Butler Bass, Diana. *Grateful: The Transformative Power of Giving Thanks.* San Francisco, California: HarperOne, 2018.
Carothers, Merlin. *Power in Praise.* Merlin Carothers, 1980.
Cousins, Norman. *Anatomy of an Illness, 2nd edition.* New York City, New York: W. W. Norton and Company, 2001.
Kaufman, Neil Barry. *Happiness is a Choice.* New York City, New York: Ballantine Books, 1994.

Lectio Divina with Scripture

Hall, Thelma. *Too Deep for Words: Rediscovering Lectio Divina.* New York City, New York: Paulist Press, 1988
Merrill, Nan. *Psalms for Praying: An Invitation to Wholeness.* New York City, New York: Continuum, 2006.
Smith, Martin. *The Word is Very Near You: A Guide to Praying with Scripture.* Boston, Massachusetts: Cowley Publications, 1989.
Stahl, Carolyn. *Opening to God: Guided Imagery for Meditation on Scripture for Individuals and Groups.* Nashville, Tennessee: The Upper Room, 1977.

Lectio Divina with Nature

Cannato, Judy. *Field of Compassion: How the New Cosmology is Transforming Spiritual Life:* Notre Dame, Indiana: Sorin Books, 2010.
Cannato, Judy. *Radical Amazement: Contemplative Lessons from Black Holes, Supernovas, and other Wonders of the Universe.* Notre Dame, Indiana, Sorin Books: 2006.
Fischer, Kathleen. *Loving Creation. Christian Spirituality, Earth-Centered and Just.* Mahwah, New Jersey: Paulist Press, 2009. "Sacred Reading of the Book of Nature" pp.117-120.

Hamma, Robert M. *Earth's Echo: Sacred Encounters with Nature.* Notre Dame, Indiana: Sorin Books, 2002.

May, Gerald. *The Wisdom of the Wilderness. Experiencing the Healing Power of Nature.* San Francisco, California: Harper, 2006.

Newell, J. Phillip. *Sounds of the Eternal.* (Audio CD) Material Media: 2011.

Swimme, Brian. *The Hidden Heart of Cosmos: Humanity and the New Story.* New York City, New York: Orbis Books, 1996.

Mindful Meals

Bays, Jan Chosen. *Mindful Eating: A Guide to Rediscovering a Healthy and Joyful Relationship with Food (Revised Edition).* Boulder, Colorado: Shambhala Press, 2017.

Hanh, Thich Nhat. *Savor: Mindful Eating, Mindful Life.* San Francisco, California: HarperOne, 2011.

Lindstorm, Simeon. *Mindful Eating: A Healthy, Balanced and Compassionate Way to Stop Overeating, How to Lose Weight and Get a Real Taste of Life by Eating Mindfully.* CreateSpace, 2014.

Community Rituals

Rupp, Joyce. *Praying our Goodbyes.* Notre Dame, Indiana: Ave Maria Press, 2012.

Taize. *Songs and Prayers from Taize: Keyboard Accompaniment,* Chicago, Illinois: GIA Publications, 1994.

Contemplative Living

Cooper, David. *Solitude, Simplicity and Silence.* New York City, New York: Bell Tower, 1991.

Edwards, Tilden. *Living in the Presence: Disciplines for the Spiritual Heart.* San Francisco, California: Harper & Row, 1995.

Edwards, Tilden. *Embracing the Call to Spiritual Depth.* Mahwah, New Jersey: Paulist Press, 2010.

King, Ruth. *Mindful of Race: Transforming Racism from the Inside Out*. Louisville, Colorado: Sounds True, 2018.

Lawrence, Brother, 1611-1691. *The Practice of the Presence of God*. Available in the public domain at: https://www.ccel.org/ccel/lawrence/practice.txt

May, Gerald. *The Awakened Heart*. San Francisco, California: HarperOne (Reprint Edition), 1993.

May, Gerald. *The Dark Night of the Soul*. San Francisco, California: HarperCollins, 2005.

McColman, Carl. *Answering the Contemplative Call: First Steps on the Mystical Path*. Newburyport, Massachusetts: Hampton Road Publishing, 2013.

McColman, Carl. *The Big Book of Christian Mysticism: The Essential Guide to Contemplative. Spirituality*. Newburyport, Massachusetts: Hampton Road Publishing, 2010.

Wolpert, Daniel. *Creating a Life with God: The Call of Ancient Prayer Practices*. Nashville, Tennessee: Upper Room: 2003.

Multi-Faith Perspectives on Contemplative Practice

Bhagvad Gita, Chapter Six: The Yoga of Meditation.

Dalai Lama, *The Stages of Meditation (reprint edition)*. Boulder, Colorado: Snow Lion, 2003.

Khan, Hazrat Inayat. *The Inner Life*. Boulder, Colorado: Shambhala, 1997

Teasdale, Wayne. *The Mystic Heart: Discovering a Universal Spirituality in the World's Religions*, Novato, California: New World Library, 2005.

Centered Action

Amato, Nicholas. *Living in God: Contemplative Prayer and Contemplative Action*. Bloomington, Indiana: Westbow Press, 2016.

Bankston, Marjorie Zoet. *Creative Aging: Rethinking Retirement and Non-Retirement in a Changing World*. Nashville, Tennessee: Skylight

Paths, 2010.

Bolles, Richard. *What Color is Your Parachute? Revised.* Berkeley, California: Ten Speed Press, 2019.

O'Connor, Elizabeth. *Journey Inward, Journey Outward.* San Francisco, California: HarperCollins, 1975

Holmes, Barbara. *Joy Unspeakable. Contemplative Practices of the Black Church.* Minneapolis, Minnesota: Fortress Press, 2nd Edition, 2017.

Other Works Cited

Berry, Thomas. *The Dream of the Earth,* Oakland, California: Sierra Club Books, 1988.

Berry, Thomas. *The Great Work: Our Way into the Future.* New York City, New York: Broadway Books, 2000.

Buechner, Frederick. *Wishful Thinking: A Seeker's ABC.* San Francisco, California: HarperOne, 1993.

Flinchbaugh, Nancy. *Letters from the Earth.* Springfield, Ohio: Higher Ground Books and Media, 2018).

Flinchbaugh, Nancy. *Revelation at the Labyrinth.* Little Elm, Texas: eLectio Publishing, 2017.

Macy, Joanna and Chris Brownstone. *Active Hope: How to Face the Mess We're in without Going Crazy.* Novato, California: New World Library, 2012.

Merton, Thomas. The Sign of Jonas. New York: Harcourt, Brace & Co., 1953.

Newell, J. Phillip. *Sounds of the Eternal.* Audio CD, 2011.

Taylor-Stinson, Therese. *"Silence and the Oppressed." Next Church Blog,* https://nextchurch.net/silence-and-the-oppressed/, 2019.

Other Resources

Shalem Institute for Spiritual Formation in Washington, D.C., offers programs on leading contemplative small groups and retreats, spiritual direction training, training for clergy and other seminars and retreats. www.shalem.org

Labyrinth Websites: www.labyrinth.org, labyrinthlocator.com, thelabyrinthsociety.org

Finger labyrinth websites

Devozine.upperoom.org/spiritual-practices/praying-with-a-finger-labyrinth

Labyrinth society.org > download-a-labyrinth

Heatherplett.com > 2015/01 > make-finger-labyrinth-also-piece-of-art

The Spirituality Network in Columbus, Ohio offers many retreats and workshops. www.spiritualitynetwork.org

Dayspring Retreat Center in Germantown, MD offers wonderful silent retreats. www.dayspringretreat.org

Acknowledgements

I would like to first acknowledge the many people who have guided me on my personal path of awakening. I am so grateful to my parents, Rev. Dr. James and Jean Flinchbaugh, who nurtured me in a Christian home and church. And to the other pastors and friends at Belmont United Methodist Church in Dayton, Ohio, where I first chose a spiritual path for my life and began my faith journey, leading me to Otterbein College in Westerville, Ohio, where I studied religion and sociology, growing in both faith, knowledge and practice. I am grateful for Rev. Dr. Gary Putnam and my friends and students at the Ames Wesley Foundation at Iowa State University where I led campus ministry groups and retreats in my twenties. I remember Howard Martin, teaching contemplative practice in Iowa City at the Presbyterian Church and the brothers of Taize, who journeyed to Iowa City to lead a retreat I attended. I am also so grateful for the spiritual directors who have guided me through my mid life into the present, including Marie Andre-Dufour, Victoria Burke, Nancy Nikiforow and Loretta Farmer.

In my thirties, I remember growing in prayer and relationship in the small groups of San Antonio Mennonite Church, with Pastor Don and Jan Rheinheimer and many other young parents. In my forties, I found a small group at First Lutheran Church Springfield with Gundula Houff, Jan Kulisek, Donna Clark, Barb Kaiser, Jeanne Imhoff, Shirley Wuchter, and Holly Wolfe, where we read contemplative books, prayed and laughed together. In my fifties, I was blessed with attending the Shalem Institute for Spiritual Formation's Leading Contemplative Small Groups and Retreats led by Ann Dean, and my peer group leader, Trish Stefanik. Later, I participated in becoming a Labyrinth Facilitator in a class led by Lauren Artress of Veriditas at Harmony Farms in Dayton, Ohio.

I am particularly grateful to Trinity Lutheran Church in Vermilion, Ohio, and my friends there, Gundula and the late Rev. Larry

Houff, who invited me to lead a contemplative retreat. This book started in preparation for sharing the weekend with them. And I also thank my current church, First Baptist Springfield, who invited me to lead contemplative offerings during our women's annual retreat, which has helped me refine some of these sessions, and the Adult Forum class my husband and I taught on Christian Responsibility with the Earth, which included Lectio Divina with the Earth. And I thank our church's Labyrinth Walkers group that also has continued to provide labyrinth experiences with me for our community.

In terms of developing the book, I'm grateful to my writing coach, Kathie Giorgio, for encouragement and guidance. I appreciate Therese Taylor-Stinson's counsel on the many faces of contemplation for people of color and Winkie Mitchell who introduced me to Ruth King's work. Also, I thank my husband, Steve Schlather, for his copy editing and ongoing support and encouragement for me and my writing life. Finally, I thank Rebecca Benston of Higher Ground Books and Media for welcoming my book and working with me to prepare the final copy.

Most of all, I am thankful to God for loving me from my childhood through the many journeys of my life. Our Creator leads me into such deep places of meaning, joy, service and action. Our God loves me like a father and a mother and writes letters to me under her pen name of Gaia, guiding me on the path of my days. Her love is ever-renewing, ever-enlightening, ever-amazing. I am so grateful for my spiritual path.

Other titles from Higher Ground Books & Media:

Wise Up to Rise Up by Rebecca Benston

A Path to Shalom by Steen Burke

For His Eyes Only by John Salmon, Ph.D.

Miracles: I Love Them by Forest Godin

32 Days with Christ's Passion by Mark Etter

Shameless Persistence by Sandra Bretting

Out of Darkness by Stephen Bowman

Breaking the Cycle by Willie Deeanjlo White

Healing in God's Power by Yvonne Green

Despising the Shame by Talia Stone

The Real Prison Diaries by Judy Frisby

Add these titles to your collection today!

http://www.highergroundbooksandmedia.com

Do you have a story to tell?

Higher Ground Books & Media is an independent Christian-based publisher specializing in stories of triumph! Our purpose is to empower, inspire, and educate through the sharing of personal experiences.

Please visit our website for our submission guidelines.

http://www.highergroundbooksandmedia.com

Made in USA - North Chelmsford, MA
1114445_9781949798623
05.21.2020 1414